"A necessary wake-up call! We [...]
questions, as part of honest and [...]
broad range of voices, to avoid sleepwalking
into an inhuman future."
Ed Greig, Chief Disruptor, Deloitte

"Dizzying, provocative and smart analysis on what should matter
to humankind, today and tomorrow. Factual, contemporary and
realistic, this story encourages positive thinking about the decisions
we must take to deliver on the promise of a better future."
Martin Jetter, Chairman, IBM Europe, Middle East & Africa

"*The Future Starts Now* offers diverse narratives of the future:
positive and negative, fearful and hopeful, social and technological.
In particular, by emphasizing social change and empowering to
shape our own future in the present, it provides a
contemporary view of foresight."
Tanja Schindler, Futurist and Founder, Futures Space

"Whether you are pessimistic or optimistic about the future... read
this book!"
Boris Veldhuijzen van Zanten, Founder & CEO, TNW

"With excellent essays exploring topics as diverse as education and
Mars, this is an inspirational read for anyone aspiring for
a pragmatic utopia!"
Stefan Ferber, Co-CEO & CTO, Bosch.IO

"Humanity is suffering from a dangerous short-termism and risking
the well-being of future generations. This book is like a message
from the future with a call to action to change our behaviour.
Recommended reading for everyone that wants to
create a better future."
**Matthew Timms, Chief Technology Officer
and CEO, E.ON Digital**

"A mind-blowing journey that challenges the reader, with essays
both fascinating and challenging. After all, what is the future we
desire, we deserve ... and are willing to work towards?"
Michael Dolbec, Executive Managing Director, GE Ventures

THE FUTURE STARTS NOW

THEO PRIESTLEY
AND
BRONWYN WILLIAMS

EXPERT INSIGHTS INTO THE FUTURE OF BUSINESS, TECHNOLOGY AND SOCIETY

BLOOMSBURY BUSINESS
LONDON • OXFORD • NEW YORK • NEW DELHI • SYDNEY

BLOOMSBURY BUSINESS
Bloomsbury Publishing Plc
50 Bedford Square, London, WC1B 3DP, UK
29 Earlsfort Terrace, Dublin 2, Ireland

BLOOMSBURY, BLOOMSBURY BUSINESS and the Diana logo are trademarks
of Bloomsbury Publishing Plc

First published in Great Britain 2021

A catalogue record for this book is available from the British Library

Library of Congress Cataloguing-in-Publication data has been applied for

ISBN: 978-1-4729-8150-9; eBook: 978-1-4729-8151-6

2 4 6 8 10 9 7 5 3 1

Typeset by Deanta Global Publishing Services, Chennai, India
Printed and bound in Great Britain by CPI Group (UK) Ltd, Croydon CR0 4YY

MIX
Paper from
responsible sources
FSC® C020471

To find out more about our authors and books visit www.bloomsbury.com
and sign up for our newsletters

Contents

Foreword by Darren Roos

I'd actually never thought much about the future. Like many of us, I was focused on next month, next quarter or perhaps my next holiday. As I got older and more career oriented, I extended that a few years to include my next job and the planning that was required. This meant thinking about my CV, my education, my title and my roles. But that was it. Beyond this was a place in time that I would deal with when I got there because, frankly, I couldn't influence it. One day I got a call from Theo inviting me to do a TED talk and, in preparation, I started to think about 'the future' in the context of my son Luke, who was seven at the time. I reflected on how the future would impact his education, what kind of world he would live in, how he would date and meet his future partner and the type of job he would have. It was a wakeup call as it dawned on me that I had been oblivious to this uncertain reality that I would inevitably live through. What will my life look like in the future?

This realization brought about an awareness that, while I couldn't necessarily have a meaningful impact on the future, I could definitely prepare for whatever this future may bring. Along with this reflection came a new interest in the concept of futurists and their diverse views of what the future will hold. Some things are undeniable: the future is coming, we don't know exactly what it will look like, and the further out you look the less certain it is. But, irrespective of what the future brings, understanding the trajectory we are moving on and preparing ourselves and future generations undoubtedly gives us an enormous advantage over those that simply drift towards the future. Never before has the pace of change been so fast and yet it will never again be so slow.

2020 brought with it immense change and turmoil. It shone a spotlight on the socio-economic divide, differing political value systems, growing nationalism, and climate change but most of all, it highlighted the speed with which the world can change. No longer can we reflect on the future as a point in time that may never arrive. The authors and contributors of this book provide a variety of ideas which provide valuable insights and importantly challenge the reader to think about what they believe the future will bring. *The Future Starts Now* shows how futurism is now more relevant than ever, and is the best preparation that we have for the future.

Darren Roos, CEO, IFS

Foreword by Jon Christian

When people learn that I'm an editor for an online publication called *Futurism*, they often ask me what I think the future is going to be like.

'I don't know,' I usually reply. 'After all, it hasn't happened yet.'

This is a lazy dodge, obviously, but it's a very tricky question. Most people are terrible at predicting the future. Occasionally someone gets lucky and anticipates something more or less accurately decades before it happens – think E.M. Forster's ominous novella *The Machine Stops*, which envisioned something very much like the internet back in 1909 – but most people who try end up being embarrassingly wrong.

Personally, though I've always been fascinated by visions of the future, I have no urge to add to this sprawling graveyard of failed predictions. The way I look at it, the only thing journalists who cover the future have the power to do is to hunt for futuristic things that are already cropping up here in the present, and then report them as we would any other story: factually, contextually, and with a healthy dose of scepticism.

That's a philosophy, I was encouraged to find, that is on full display in *The Future Starts Now*. You will find it not just in the chapters authored by the book's many thoughtful and qualified contributors, but also in Theo and Bronwyn's core proposition that the entire notion of predicting a specific, deterministic future is flawed from the get-go. Instead, in a framing they call 'anti-futurist' – a snappy neologism I may start using myself – they argue that it's worth mapping out a plethora of potential futures precisely so that we may do battle, here in the present, to encourage the good outcomes and deter the bad ones.

That's not a silver bullet – some readers are surely going to disagree about which futures are desirable, after all – but it is a heartening and pragmatic message for the dismal historical moment that we currently find ourselves in. An awful pandemic has swept the globe, reminding us that we still have little control over nature's most chaotic processes, and even less over our own worst impulses toward misinformation and inequity. The environment seems to be degrading at such a speed that even the most optimistic projections doubt whether we are past the point of no return. Corporations appear to be amassing the power of minor gods, and with none of the wisdom or benevolence we might expect from traditional deities.

I should point out that, even though those types of broad-spectrum, civilization-shaking questions about the future are unquestionably important, they can also feel theoretical and remote from our everyday experiences. As journalists like myself are painfully aware, the future-oriented topics that attract the most popular attention tend to be farfetched and unorthodox, like sex robots and longevity treatments and space colonization.

That's not to say these more salacious stories are unimportant, but treating them constructively requires a steady editorial hand – and this collection pulls off a prestigious move by delicately touching upon such topics in order to draw readers into larger conversations about more pressing and significant concerns. And rest assured that it's never dull; the essays herein indeed grapple with everything from rarefied economic questions to virtual sex appeal and space explosions, all of which I'm sure will be at least somewhat relevant as the actual future unfolds.

As it threads that needle between the accessible and the rarefied, a recurring theme in this book is that the seeds of our destruction are often closely linked with our best hopes. Genetic science may allow tomorrow's terrorists to create terrifying bioweapons, but it also helped physicians develop COVID-19 vaccines in record time.

Advances in automation could eliminate the livelihoods of workers and consolidate power in the hands of megacorporations, or they could let us construct a fairer society that liberates everybody to do what they love.

Dazzled yet? Frankly, it breaks my little journalist brain. With all apologies to W.B. Yeats, I've started getting a sense that we're all turning and turning in various widening gyres, and it's difficult to imagine that this will last forever. At worst, I fear a rapid arms race between the good and bad uses of new technologies that will eventually escalate to some terrible and apocalyptic conclusion. At best, perhaps we'll discover some new sense of equilibrium – and maybe, if we're lucky and listen to our better angels, it'll be one that nudges the world in a gentler and more prosperous direction.

It's also worth noting that the future, by necessity, needs to deal with the past. This book spills a good deal of ink, both explicitly and implicitly, about the legacy of cyberpunk, a speculative fiction subgenre characterized by an ambivalent relationship toward capitalism and a penchant toward 'used futures' with messy, evocative histories. I won't muddy the waters further except to agree that whatever future our children inherit, it will never represent a tabula rasa. Instead, like every future before it ossified into the present and eventually receded into the past, it will surely be built on the rubble of everything that came before it.

Suffice to say that I enjoyed the book, and I hope you will too – and that the next time someone asks me about the future, I may have a new answer.

'I'm not sure,' I might say. 'But there's a new essay collection you might want to check out.'

Jon Christian, freelance journalist
and news editor at *Futurism*

Introduction

The choices we make today – as individuals, as businesses, and as members of society – ripple out all around us, amplifying over time. What will future generations – our children and our grandchildren (indeed, even our future selves, should we live long enough) – make of the choices we are making on their behalf?

The truth is, the future is not fixed: it is neither as bleak as the prophets of doom predict, nor as shiny and brilliant as the optimistic smooth-talking 'singularity' soothsayers promise. Despite what powerful, power-hungry politicians and high-profile, profit-hungry business personalities tell us, nothing is inevitable, except for death and taxes (and even then, advances in extreme longevity science and radical economic models could feasibly change that in the not too distant future).

This means that exponential growth is not guaranteed; universal basic income is not the *only* solution to surviving the robot uprising; moving to a Mars colony is not the only way to save the human race from climate change; you will probably never own a flying car; and submitting to an omniscient surveillance state is not the only way to protect our babies from the big bad world outside.

We can surely do better than these limited overly optimistic and overly pessimistic visions will have us believe.

We also have the power to change *the future of the future* to a future that works for more of us.

That is why we have gathered together a carefully selected group of disillusioned futurists from all over the world to bring you this book, as both an apology to future generations – and a warning to our own.

This book is designed to get us thinking about the futures we *don't* want to live in, as well as those that we *do* want to create – and to suggest some actionable solutions we can implement today to make sure we end up in the future we want for ourselves, our careers, our businesses, our societies, and our dependents.

Now, the future needs *you*.

Letters from the Editors

HAUNTED BY HAUNTOLOGY

When I first envisioned this book, it was meant to be a series of statements of apology, written from the perspective of a future self and sent back in time to a younger generation, for the mistakes we've made and how not to repeat them. This seemed like a logical framework and solid idea but was ultimately doomed to become a very long-winded and regretful monologue.

The next idea came from discovering the term 'hauntology' in reference to the future.

Hauntology (haunting + ontology), a term coined by the French philosopher Jacques Derrida, is the feeling or lamentation for futures that we were promised but which have never materialized – lost futures, in a sense. As futurists, we often hear people ask, 'Where are the flying cars and jetpacks we were promised?' (fellow futurist Doug Vining explores this concept further in Chapter 10) and this is a typical pop-culture view of something that has generally been accepted as a window to the future, or certainly one possible future. Somehow, many optimistic predictions and inventions touted during the late 1930s and early 1940s at the famous World's Fair exhibition, Futurama, have been lost to time and as a result we feel like we were robbed of a brighter tomorrow. Hence, hauntology, and a sense of lost opportunities.

Again, though, an entire book dedicated to listing all our undelivered potential wouldn't make for very positive reading.

However, after chatting through some ideas with Bronwyn one afternoon, via a ropy Skype connection, about the overall concept and goal for the book, we both came to the conclusion that in order to tackle something of this magnitude and diversity we would need the input of people of equal magnitude and diversity of thought in order to deliver something valuable to the reader – something that wasn't written from a singular point of view or with an overabundance of misery.

And so *The Future Starts Now* was born: a book that examines the future from multiple perspectives, and through the diverse voices of many amateur and professional futurists alike. We invited a roster of very different people, across different continents, to cover topics they felt strongly about that touched upon the main themes: how will our current paths and ideals affect business, society and technology, and what can we do to learn from them?

This book is a journey, the futurist's version of Homer's *Odyssey* or Chaucer's *The Canterbury Tales*.

It will develop your understanding of the impact of changes and how these ripple into the future and whether these possible futures are good, bad or somewhere in-between.

It will leave you questioning what you see around you today, and will hopefully galvanize your thinking and motivation to change the world around you for the better.

It provides rich insight from people you may never have heard of before, and will leave you wanting to discover more from them as a result.

Above all else, it is meant to change how you view the future and persuade you that, with the right frame of mind and tools at your side, you too can envision and work towards a better one.

The future does indeed start now, and it starts with you.

Theo Priestley, 2021

THE INERTIA OF POSTALGIA

Postalgia is a term used by science fiction writer William Gibson to explain the *future fatigue* plaguing contemporary culture.

Postalgia is similar to nostalgia; however, where nostalgia is a hankering after the lost past, postalgia is a hankering after the transient present. Postalgia is, in other words, the sense that things right now are as good as they will ever get.

This increasingly prevalent pessimistic world view is the *result* of the long slow decline in productivity and equality of progress we have seen in much of the developed world in recent decades. It is the result of the hopelessness of postmodernism; the pointlessness of existence without belief in anything beyond the here and now; the trap of being caught in the endless *now*. Postalgia is the curse of a civilization without a past it can be proud of and without a future worth believing in; a society left without any unifying grand narrative to follow or substantial positive vision to work towards.

However, I firmly believe that the inertia of postalgia can be defeated with *pragmatic optimism* about the future of humanity. And it was this belief that the future not only can but *has to* be better (not just bigger, mind you, but really better) than the present that drove me to work with Theo to put this book together. It was this simple thought that sent

5

us on a virtual journey around the world to find more like-minded futurists and anti-futurists who both understand the very real problems facing the world and have some rather interesting ideas about what we can do to fix them.

This rather practical view of the future deviates from mainstream shiny pop futurism (of the sort that has popularized the fairy tales of never-ending exponential growth) and instead involves exploring pragmatic *protopias*, which recognize that perfect utopias are a mirage. Designing protopias requires us to recognize the limitations of our own brilliance, and to replace the idea of what is *perfect* for you or me with more *practical and inclusive* shared future ideas. This in turn means we need to understand the potential dangers of current trends and trajectories; use foresight to extrapolate the intended and unintended consequences of our pet policies and favoured choices; and stretch our imaginations to explore the limits of possible, preferable alternatives.

Right now, the world is desperate for good public and private sector leaders with clear – and desirable – visions of what the future could and should be. Humans have a deep desire for something worth believing in, something worth working towards, something worth building together. This means the future is a huge source of competition for individuals and organizations with the courage and the competence to both imagine it and inspire others to help them build it. The future has to be imagined and articulated before it can be actualized. I believe that, with enough of us doing that imagining and articulating, we can come up with some better ideas than the ones currently lying around.

Of course, this vacuum of new and interesting future ideas is both an opportunity and a threat. It is certainly an opportunity, because as the future is uncharted territory, it is open for anyone to claim. This means that your ideas of the future – should they be big and bold enough – have, in theory, as much a chance of changing the world as anyone else's. At the same time, however, it is a threat, in that the future is constantly at risk of being hijacked by the personal agendas of powerful corporations and individuals. Since one person's idea of utopia could very well be your or my idea of a perfect dystopia, it is imperative that we include more individuals, more communities and more companies in conversations about where the world is heading, and if this is, indeed, where we want to go at all. Human progress is a team sport. More perspectives result in more ideas to solve the world's wicked problems. More collaborative conscious design of preferable futures that address the unique needs of individuals and communities will result in more stable and more sustainable societies and more equitably distributed progress for humanity.

This means everyone, including you, can (indeed should) become a futurist and begin to explore the limits of what is possible and what is preferable for you, your organization, your communities, your nation, and for human civilization at large.

Although professional futurists like myself and the other authors you will meet in this book can and do use tools, models and facilitation techniques to help organizations to make sense of the future and our place in it, you do not require a degree in future studies or official certification to become a futurist. All you require is an enquiring mind, the courage to ask questions, and the willingness to let go of the probable in order to imagine the possible. Not only that, but small actions and ideas can also have a massive impact on future realities. This means that individual choices can and do change the future. This in turn means that not only can you change the future, but it is your duty to do so if you do believe the direction in which the world is heading is *not* where you want to end up.

Right now, there has never been a more important time to define and design your own preferable future. The stakes have never been higher. There are more people than ever before on planet Earth (and people have always been the primary drivers of progress and change). Technology has progressed to the point that we have the power to destroy ourselves and our planet with weapons of mass destruction and reckless consumption habits (as Leah Zaidi describes in Chapter 2); or to reinvent ourselves by changing the very course of the evolution of our species (as Craig Wing explains in Chapter 20). We have the power to drive ourselves into extinction, and to bring long-extinct species back from the dead. We collectively have the ability to decide on what world we are going to create for future generations to inherit.

If we want to change the future for the better, we need more people discussing more ideas, not the same old ideas from the same old voices – and that requires being informed about the biggest questions of our age. As such, in this book, we have sought out the world's most important future voices; some of whom are well known, others of whom are less well known – but all of whom have a unique perspective on the biggest challenges facing the global community right now. The individuals we have chosen represent different communities around the world and come from very different educational and professional backgrounds. What they have in common is that they are all *independent* voices, beholden to no one other than their own conscience. We invited each of these futurists to share their uncensored thoughts in the form of an essay designed to stimulate thoughts about the future, and more importantly to inspire us to action to change the future for the better.

After all, a futurist's role is not to predict the future, so much as it is to *change* the future. Good futurists extrapolate trends to illuminate the full scope of potential dangers and opportunities ahead and inspire others to take action to divert the future from what is most likely to occur towards what is most desirable for the most people. (Indeed, if a futurist successfully predicts the future, that futurist has probably failed to do their job.)

Hopefully, reading this book will both inspire and scare you in equal measure. If we have done our job, then the very act of reading these essays will change the future that we have described.

Bronwyn Williams, 2021

PART ONE

Dark Mirrors

Nothing is real and everything is possible. Life is becoming untethered from reality.

From an economic perspective, value has been decoupled from real-world resources. Wealth is becoming decoupled from scarcity, with massively destabilizing effects. On the one hand, this decoupling of wealth and real-world resources could see us headed for debt, default, overshoot, and economic and environmental collapse. On the other hand, as value and economic growth sever more and more of their ties with physical resources, limits to growth, tied to energy production, pollution costs and scarce minerals, water and land, seem to fall away. As long as we are prepared to suspend our disbelief and believe in the value of intangible assets the same way that we currently believe in the value of tangible assets, we can, perhaps, have our planet (without destroying it) and our economic growth too. In theory, could we transcend our limits to growth if 'value' can be created in virtual worlds from virtual currencies without being constrained by reality?

From a socio-political perspective: Facts have become relative, science has become personal, and truth has become optional, rather than absolute. White lies are perpetuated by powerful voices as facts, such as the idea that surveillance is necessary for security – that liberty requires increased state control – or that perpetual war in the Middle East is necessary for 'peace' back 'home' in the West, or that perpetually increasing disposable consumer culture is the only way to achieve 'progress'. Such assertions are Orwellian and are designed to make us question our own sanity. It's the final form of gaslighting, conducted on a scale hitherto undreamt of.

From a cultural perspective: The present has become untethered from the past and the future. This is because, as deepfake technologies improve, they now have the ability to manipulate the past as well as the future. We can no longer be sure that a historical document, photograph, or even video footage has not been manipulated to change history (in ways not even Orwell's Big Brother could have imagined). Whether historical or modern, every piece of media is increasingly becoming subject to manipulation – allowing for a widespread obfuscation of fact and fiction.

Whether historical or modern, every piece of media is increasingly becoming subject to intricate manipulation – allowing for a widespread obfuscation of fact and fiction. As such, it is not implausible that future generations will question almost every historical fact we take for granted today.

Did the atrocities of the Second World War and the Eastern Bloc communist experiments of the 20th century really play out the way we were taught in school? Did the Rwandan genocide really happen in the happy-go-lucky 1990s? Deepfaked history will allow future humans to question the unquestionable and rewrite our perspective according to the whims of the current 'thought leaders' (or thought police, depending on whether they find themselves living in free or totalitarian societies) in real time, and that of course is the difference. We know, of course, that history has *always* been written and rewritten by the current victors; what is different this time is rather the speed at which history can be edited, erased and weaponized to manipulate the future course of history by sowing miss and disinformation to catalyze social unrest, in real time, undermining the trust upon which any successful society is built.

Already, the only truth, the only real point in time we, as individuals, can be even relatively sure of, is the lived now. The past is a foreign country that erases itself behind us. The future is an unknowable land.

When history becomes as mysterious and fluid as the future, and only the endless, personal, *now* makes any sense at all, what becomes of society?

What becomes of a civilization completely untethered from time and perspective?

How can a community build a shared future without a shared past?

How can we have clear foresight without hindsight to guide us?

Surely we are doomed to repeat our most miserable mistakes if we cannot remember them?

Of course, all these untethered ideas rely on us believing in them – against the evidence of our senses – in order for them to continue to exist.

How long will our belief in the impossible, yet socially and financially necessary, hold?

And what happens when it fails?

In this section, which we have titled *Dark Mirrors*, our authors take you on a journey to the (still preventable) dystopias that could await us as we explore the limits to growth and social stability. They look at what *could go wrong* if we lose touch with what is real and human in favour of the artificial; and what *could go right* as we attempt to *transcend* the boundaries of what is physically possible and socially desirable to a more sustainable, more sensible future.

After reading this section, we would encourage you to conduct a 'Dark Mirror' audit on your own organization to explore what could go wrong and what you can do now to start putting it right again.

Such an audit involves assessing your business for any and all possible dystopian outcomes in order to identify and course-correct any unintended consequences of your actions that could have long-term negative effect on society, the economy, or the environment. This includes, but is not limited to:

- assessing unsustainable resource consumption and waste disposal practices;
- identifying human rights abuses by supply chain partners;
- identifying if the technology you use or develop could (inadvertently or not) harm any living beings;
- making sure you are not violating privacy or engaging in ethically questionable manipulation tactics such as 'fake news' or 'nudge marketing'.

Start with Dystopia

By Nikolas Badminton, global futurist,
researcher, speaker and media commentator

Powerful, terrifying and entertaining stories have seeped into popular culture and are now being propagated through mainstream media, blogs, podcasts and social media as being the forewarning of modern society out of control. But, as we find in this chapter, we can start by thinking of dystopia as a starting point for dreaming up and actualizing more positive futures for all.

Futurism itself is born from ideas of dystopia – a twisted world that doesn't exist but is a symbol of human endeavour gone wrong, or challenged in a way in which we have little or no control.

True dystopias are fantastical and unbelievable – Iceland being ripped apart by seismic and volcanic activity, thus causing total population displacement and the end of the physical land mass; a meteor destroying Washington, DC, and crippling the United States administration and leadership; the sudden death of all livestock globally and the collapse of food supply chains. I could go on. Basically, dystopias are the absolute worst situations we can imagine. They are incredibly useful to explore as they nullify yesterday's logic and open our minds to completely new and unexpected territories for creating a resilient world.

FROM ESCHATOLOGICAL BEGINNINGS
TO THE SINGULARITY

The Oxford English Dictionary identifies the earliest use of the term 'futurism' in English as 1842, to refer, in a theological context, to the Christian eschatological tendency of that time (specifically referring to the Book of Revelation, the Book of Ezekiel and the Book of Daniel as future events in a literal, physical, apocalyptic and global context). Death, judgement, and the final destiny of the soul and humankind are central themes and were deployed to incite fear and control.

If we look at the Bible's apocalyptic prophecy held in the Book of Revelation 21:4, it provides an example of powerful eschatological short storytelling:

And death shall be no more, neither shall there be mourning nor crying nor pain any more.

The dystopian threat here is that everything is utterly gone. Yet there are positive aspects of this future that are circumscribed by the negative aspects of the present. Its purpose is to strengthen the faith of the members of the churches by giving to them the assurance that deliverance from the evil powers arrayed against them was close at hand.

A more modern and technologically driven idea is that the accelerating rate of scientific progress will lead to a 'singularity' – a hypothetical future where technological growth becomes uncontrollable and irreversible, resulting in unforeseeable changes to human civilization. Human 2.0, upgraded with implanted machinery to enhance intelligence, strength and capability. A future that would profoundly and unpredictably change the course of human history and result in the line being blurred between *Homo sapiens* and machines.

It's a blunt tool. As futurists, we need to forgo this 'open and shut' approach towards a more foresight-driven exploration of all aspects of the dystopia, and the myriad of associated outcomes.

DYSTOPIAN INSPIRATIONS: BLACK SWANS AND ELEPHANTS

As a futurist, I have a penchant for 'black swans'. I'm not talking about the generally ill-tempered, unwieldy and aloof yet elegant birds, although they share a lot with the metaphorical 'black swans' presented by philosopher Nicholas Taleb.

His idea of 'black swans' is events that appear seemingly from nowhere and have a surprising effect. Such 'black swan' events range from the disruptions caused by the personal computer and the Internet to unexpected terrorist attacks in new jurisdictions, meteorite crashes, and even alien invasions.

When they occur, these events all have major, irreversible impacts – systematic, geopolitical, cultural, psychological, societal, physical – that are often inappropriately rationalized afterwards with the benefit of hindsight and retrospective analysis. When we use strategic foresight to potentially identify future 'black swans', we can uncover weaknesses in our systems and frailties in our society and highlight the myriad points of potential failure. It is then that we have the opportunity to galvanize our strategic foresight and planning and identify the full spectrum of risks.

For me, black swans are true dystopia. Not events like the 2020 pandemic (SARS-CoV-2), or 'The Great Pause', as some are romantically calling it. The threat of a pandemic similar to this one was not unknown to governments or risk analysts; indeed numerous foresight practitioners predicted the likelihood of such an event. The shock is that it was completely underestimated and any plans were so surface level that every government started from ignorance and denial, then emerged with poorly planned responses. Rather, the 2020 pandemic was a 'black elephant' with all the traits of a black swan: global disruption, deaths, and rolling wildly out of control while we scrambled to try and work out what this invisible foe was. Could it be true that it had been waiting to happen for over a century? Well, we had the 1918 Spanish flu pandemic that claimed the lives of an estimated 20 to 50 million lives worldwide, the 'Hong Kong flu' in the 1960s, and HIV, H1N1, SARS, MERS, Zika and Ebola, which have been staring us in the face over the past three or four decades. We even had Bill Gates deliver a TED Talk in 2015 called 'The Next Outbreak? We're not Ready'.[1]

The pandemic certainly felt dystopian but even so, I don't believe it reached the scale that would drive us to make the necessary plans and precautions for future black swan events.

DESIGNING DYSTOPIAS

As futurists, we design all kinds of futures so that we can backcast effects and identify their impacts on today. The most potent futures we should recognize are dystopias. Why?

---

[1] Bill Gates, 'The Next Outbreak? We're Not Ready', TED2015. Available from: www.ted.com/talks/bill_gates_the_next_outbreak_we_re_not_ready?language=en

Because we have become aware that today's strategies are failing us as they are obsolete the moment they are established.

World leaders, governments, organizations and associations are always playing catch-up by only looking a few months or a couple of years ahead through the election cycle. In most cases they are trying to keep their heads above water and swim within the Overton window, in which accepted opinion lives within boundaries defined by policy and consensus by the lawmakers and politicians. Too often we are told to operate in a way that is acceptable, agreeable and viable.

With this in mind, we futurists are driven to go beyond those limits and be more creative. Creative with our thinking, our planning and our storytelling, so that we create a habitat to live outside of all of the boxes. It's then that we can imagine into the realm of turbulence. The modern business philosopher Peter F. Drucker truly identifies the importance of dealing with turbulence, of which dystopia is an enabler:

> The greatest danger in times of turbulence is not the turbulence itself, but to act with yesterday's logic.

We use many foresight techniques to stare into the vastness of unknown futures – all while breaking the ideas of yesterday's logic and expectations and reprogramming ourselves to expect the extreme events that are defined by dystopias.

To start defining a dystopian world, I focus on a number of techniques that allow us to quickly and effectively create dystopian futures and provoke clients to create plans to address them. I generally start with the 'Futures Cone' model as presented by Joseph Voros (it was adapted from earlier thinking by Charles Taylor in 1990, and subsequently built on thinking by Trevor Hancock and Clement Bezold in 1994: see fig. 1):

FIGURE 1   Joseph Voros' Futures Cone[2]

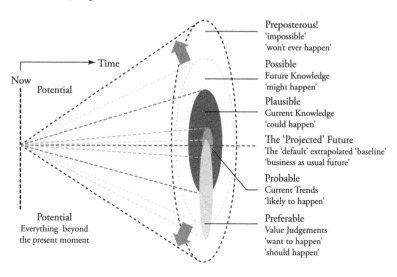

The Futures Cone is useful because it allows us to define our 'now' and then explore multiple future states. It provides us with a widened perspective that is necessary for predicting black swans. Voros has written and explored its use extensively, and explains its usage, as follows:

In the Cone, time is represented as extending from some starting point at the left – in this case starting at Now, but in many cases it is more helpful to start in the past to capture trends or events that have come before the present – and continuing steadily to some point in the future. The overall futures cone is visualized and conceptualized as having stratified subcones. Across all potential futures the subcones range from the projected future (with the highest

[2]Joseph Voros, 'The Futures Cone, use and history', The Voroscope, 24 February 2017. Available from: thevoroscope.com/2017/02/24/the-futures-cone-use-and-history/

likelihood of happening), through probable, plausible, possible, and preposterous futures. An added wrinkle is defining a region of the cone as being preferable from the perspective of an individual, organization, demographic, or nation based on a set of value judgments, and perhaps independent of the degree of possibility involved: an aspirational future.

When using the Futures Cone model I tend to focus on the easy-to-consume 'possible', 'probable' and 'preferable' futures. You'll likely read about many of those futures within the pages of this book – and they will include both solid thinking and speculation. They may not appear, at first glance, to be inherently dystopian but once we see what more positive futures can be, we can then develop ideas of what 'preposterous' futures could exist – both good and bad – and start to identify and amplify negative outcomes in that futures world view.

Personally, I often choose to explore the 'preposterous'. That means we can see the 'ridiculous', 'impossible' or 'never going to happen' events, and can then immerse our thoughts in a terrible future that might be wrought on us. There's nothing more alive than a mind, government or organization that is thrust into survival mode. This leads us down one of two paths: panic mode, or a move to mobilize strategic thinking and recognize mitigation plans against foreseen risks. That's where dystopias start to take shape.

Once we have the beginnings of what our futures could be and have identified the 'preposterous', then we can think about applying principles that help with worldbuilding. In our futures work, we should aim to follow humanistic principles for a world filled with positive solutions: humanity before technology; plurality, inclusion and equity; and advancements guided by science and creativity. To further flesh out a dystopian world, we simply invert these and apply dystopian world principles:

PRINCIPLE 1 – Narrow technology leads with prescriptive solutions to create our (singular) future: Off-the-shelf, one-size-fits-all technology solutions are deployed in a plug-and-play fashion and the 'users' need to conform to that new world. This is often called 'technological colonization' as our world is locked into the way that the solution is designed, much like the gauges of railway tracks and the neat social graph boxes presented by Facebook.

PRINCIPLE 2 – Personal gain and profit for the few: Equity is discarded in favour of smaller committees (mostly made up of men) that lack empathy for the struggles in the world.

PRINCIPLE 3 – Absolute control and speculation accelerated by gut feel: Scientific fact is often discarded and those parts that must be adhered to are bent into the shapes we need in order to prove foregone hypotheses based on what the few 'feel' is right.

Just reading these principles creates a sense of anxiety in the mind of the reader. We can then map these across multiple dimensions to model their effects. The 'Seven Foundations Model'[3] from Leah Zaidi (the author of Chapter 2 in this

---

[3]Leah Zaidi, 'Building Brave New Worlds: Science Fiction and Transition Design', Ontario College of Art and Design, December 2017. Available from: www.researchgate.net/publication/321886159_Building_Brave_New_Worlds_Science_Fiction_and_Transition_Design

book) is a modern take on worldbuilding that applies what she calls the first principles of culture:

- **Artistic** – representation, expression and form;
- **Economic** – management of wealth and resources;
- **Environmental** – ecological systems, including physical and relational space;
- **Philosophical** – epistemology (theory of knowledge), metaphysics (nature of reality), value theory (ethics and morality), logic and reason, and human nature;
- **Political** – creation, maintenance and governance of entities and society;
- **Scientific and technological** – observation of and/or experiment with the natural and physical world;
- **Social** – human organization, relational dynamics of our world and systems.

The world we create using this system allows us to see the transitions needed by providing a mental model, or 'superstructure', for culture and/or society. We can then pare civilization back down to its foundations and address what is most fundamental to the dystopia we create for ourselves. Zaidi explains:

For instance, not every civilization will take the same approach to politics (e.g. a monarchy versus a democratic republic versus a council of elders, etc.) but every civilization has engaged in some form of politics or another. In contrast, not every civilization or society values science in equal measure, but even the suppression of science affects the foundation of a civilization or society, shaping its systems and people. When we strip away anything

23

that is not foundational, we can begin to minimize our reliance on existing analogies, path dependence, and continuation scenarios by taking a first principles approach to worldbuilding. Instead, we seek to reimagine our future systems in their entirety.

It may create potency, but we have to take that larger view and make it consumable to as many people as possible.

To do that we can create hyper-short stories, sometimes known as 'hypothetical scenarios'. These ask 'what if…' and apply our dystopian principles, take reference from the worldbuilding we have done, and make key situations in which society will find itself more real and visceral to the reader. The power of asking 'what if…' is that it's an invitation to be creative as we consider futures and build dystopias.

Structuring hypothetical scenarios is relatively straightforward and we can plug our speculations into the structural elements that are available, as follows:

> What if in **[year]** **[solutions x, y and z are implemented]**, which causes **[these negative and positive outcomes]** and this affects **[people, organizations, planet]** in **[a number of ways]**

For example, what if we have a world where renewable energy and electrification were paired with a hunger for more profitable models for generating and distributing energy around the world in real time. It's an incredible future that many are aiming for and technologically it will be possible and could be a true reality by approximately 2030. However, let's stop and consider how that could also lead us into a dystopian world and investigate some of the technological solutions being discussed today – say, deep geothermal – that enable a renewable energy future (a positive thought) yet create an apex between the process for establishing that capability and a large natural disaster. That could be a world-changing earthquake – 'The Big One' – that's been expected on the West Coast of the United States for decades:

> What if in **2050, deep geothermal engineering is prevalent in California**, which causes **a series of cataclysmic seismic reactions that trigger a magnitude 10+ earthquake**, and this **kills 3.24 million people, disables businesses, stops all transportation in and out of key transportation hubs and triggers an in-state civil war for safety, food and liberty in the face of failing state and federal governments?**

As you can see, this dystopian hypothetical scenario instils fear and loss – and creates fertile ground for the creation of more hypothetical scenarios within each part of the statement.

Through this process, and with the creation of more of these short stories, multiple dimensions of the dystopia are identified and the repertoire of these hypothetical scenarios starts to show a bigger and more terrible future.

CREATING BIGGER STORIES

When we chain hypothetical scenarios together to create a larger speculation of the futures laid out before us, we have the opportunity to create a bigger story. Of course, we can stop the process with a chain of hypothetical scenarios and then move on to backcasting, strategic planning for today and risk assessment with a broader and more serious perspective. But futurists often feel that only goes part of the way and we often recommend a larger exercise of speculative design, writing and film-making to make the idea of dystopia come alive.

Stories have always been powerful tools for us futurists as they create sentimentality in the eye of the person reading or experiencing the speculative future artefact. To do this we apply the 'Hero's Journey', a concept popularized by Joseph Campbell in which the leading protagonist – or hero – is called to an adventure (see fig. 2). Weaving stories by combining hypothetical scenarios with antagonists and protagonists ultimately engages and inspires people at a deeper level.

FIGURE 2 The 'Hero's Journey', or monomyth[4]

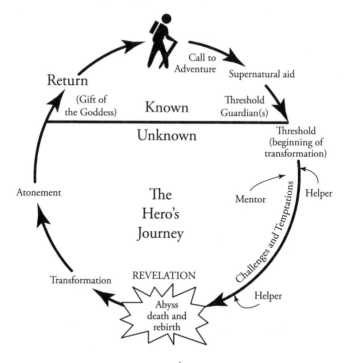

[4]'The Hero's Journey', or monomyth, Wikimedia, Public Domain. Available from: commons.wikimedia.org/wiki/File:Heroesjourney.svg

Along the way we can place helpers and guardians that assist the hero in the face of challenges and temptation. We can talk about what the 'abyss' – the deepest part of the dystopia – looks and feels like. We can identify the actions and strategies that enable transformation from the dystopian state via atonement and a triumphant return.

There are some well-known examples of how the narrative form of the hero's journey is applied in both literature and film with a view on future dystopian worlds. In 1949, the novel *1984* was released by George Orwell and showed us a future world of totalitarian control by Big Brother. It's seeped into popular culture (like many great stories) and it is often used as a reference point to the modern panopticon of big data, social media, algorithmic control and surveillance. What is interesting here is that it doesn't go through the entire cycle and the 'hero' Winston's story ends at 'transformation' and leaves an open end for the reader to imagine what comes next. I bring this up first as it's important to realize that we can apply this without completing the cycle. This is also a useful tool to encourage creative thought by the reader to extend more storytelling in the '1984 Universe'.

The next example goes full cycle and is Philip K. Dick's novella from 1956 – *The Minority Report*. Our hero is John Anderton, the creator and Head of Precrime, a police agency that taps into the visions from three mutant humans called 'precogs' to foresee and halt future crimes before they are committed. The story plays with the idea that there are three simultaneous future time paths that all exist for the pre-criminals to follow. In this he is framed, chased and eventually proves his innocence, frees the 'precogs' and the ethically questionable programme is disbanded.

Lastly, and one of my absolutely favourite visions of a cyberpunk transhumanist future, is the comic book series *Transmetropolitan*. This was written by Warren Ellis and designed by Darick Robertson from 1997 to 2002 and showed a visceral dark future of journalism, political corruption, overpopulation, a myriad of new religions, mass consumption, and the emergence of what our hero, Spider Jerusalem, called 'the new scum' of citizens as a powerful force.

Through these, and the stories we will create, readers will build deeper empathy for the hero, guardians, helpers and other players in the story. They will build stronger emotional attachments to events, objects, places, eras and beliefs within. This use of connection and sentimentality will heighten urgency with the reader.

From a longer story we can prompt the reader to raise considerations relating to challenges, opportunities and risks – and we can invite people to go further and consider them in the context of their lives and organizations.

A FINAL WORD...

When we work with governments, organizations and other leaders in the community, they often challenge us to imagine an optimistic and positive future rather than focus on fear or dystopia. Futurists certainly love to do that; to do so, however, we need to investigate all possibilities of a preposterous and dystopian future to ensure a holistic understanding, rather than a myopic and self-serving narrative that serves today and the immediate, and likely profitable, future only.

To encourage clients, we can prime the conversation about the importance of dystopias by sharing this impactful quote from author Zig Ziglar with them:

> F-E-A-R has two meanings: 'Forget Everything and Run', or, 'Face Everything and Rise'. Fear is something we all have faced, and will face again. It's inevitable, and it rears its ugly head in our life, career, or business.

There is ugliness in life today and there will be in the future. It's an anxious feeling of discomfort associated with the diligent process of investigating dystopian futures.

By starting with dystopias versus nice and convenient futures, we can establish a reality check – a clearer view of challenges ahead, identification of risks to how we operate today, and a preparation for abundant futures in the face of what might seem preposterous.

That reality check is our dystopian futures.

2

Deep Sustainability

*By Leah Zaidi, award-winning futurist and
the founder of Multiverse Design, a strategic
foresight consultancy*

Can we transcend our limits to growth? Will we run out
of ways to do more with less? Is economic growth even
compatible with sustainability? Or do we need to readjust
our expectation around human progress to fit within our
natural world without overreaching its resources. In this
essay we explore sustainability at scale and question how
to make the world more fair and equitable not just for
present humanity, but also for future generations.

We are waves from the same sea,
Leaves of the same tree,
Flowers of the same garden.[5]

---

[5]Quote shared by Xiaomi on masks sent to Italy, mistakenly attributed to Seneca.
Available from: www.newsweek.com/chinese-company-donates-tens-thousands-
masks-coronavirus-striken-italy-says-we-are-waves-1491233

Imagine you have a fever. It shows no signs of letting up. Your temperature continues to climb and each rising degree puts your life in greater danger. It's hard to breathe. You cough until your lungs ache. You have pre-existing conditions that compound the problem and might rob you of your life before the virus has a chance to take you first. You may be on your last few days.

And it's not just you, your neighbours are sick. Hundreds of thousands of others are too. Your world has come to a halt. Work is not what it used to be, there is no going outside, and all the simple pleasures you took for granted – a walk, a whiff of fresh air, that morning coffee in the local cafe – none of it is the same any more. Beyond your world, every crack in society is showing. Buried layers of poverty, abuse, isolation, racism, and a plethora of other social diseases are rising up like a flash flood, and sweeping through our once stable systems. Lying beneath the surface of fever-stricken nations is a simmering anger, a pile of kindling waiting for a match.

This chapter was written in the midst of the coronavirus (COVID-19) crisis – a worldwide disruption rooted in our relationship with nature. It is suggested that the virus first appeared in animals (bats are potential candidates), similar to how SARS first emerged in 2002, and spread to humans through wet markets in China, in which caged animals are butchered live for customers.[6,7] Far from being a black swan,

[6]World Health Organization, SARS (Severe Acute Respiratory Syndrome). Available from: www.who.int/ith/diseases/sars/en/

[7]Graham Readfearn, 'How did coronavirus start and where did it come from? Was it really Wuhan's animal market?', *Guardian*, 28 April 2020. Available from: www.theguardian.com/world/2020/apr/15/how-did-the-coronavirus-start-where-did-it-come-from-how-did-it-spread-humans-was-it-really-bats-pangolins-wuhan-animal-market

a COVID pandemic was not only predicted but anticipated by epidemiologists, foresight practitioners and other experts.[8]

Even in the early stages of the first wave, the connection between our actions and nature's response became apparent. Photos from all over the world showed significant decline in air pollution. The veil lifted on once smoggy cities as skies cleared for the first time in years. With fewer cars on the road, places as far apart as Los Angeles and Delhi boasted clean air, proving that climate change is undeniably man-made.[9]

In the years to come, we will speak of COVID-19 as a metaphor for environmental degradation, with three critical differences. First, COVID-19 was a dress rehearsal. The main event has yet to happen and, when it does, it will be the single greatest crisis humanity has ever faced. Second, there is no vaccine for the planet. Once the system tips, it will never be the same again. Third, environmental degradation is a slow process that has occurred over decades and thus is easier to dismiss. It may be years before the system collapses but that collapse could happen without warning and from an unexpected trigger.

COVID-19 required severe measures to mitigate catastrophic loss and, make no mistake, without a global shutdown, the death toll would have mounted into the millions within months. Similarly, environmental degradation will have a devastating impact.

[8]Samuel Brannen and Kathleen Hicks, 'We Predicted a Coronavirus Pandemic. Here's What Policymakers Could Have Seen Coming', *Politico*, 7 March 2020. Available from: www.politico.com/news/magazine/2020/03/07/coronavirus-epidemic-prediction-policy-advice-121172

[9]Beth Gardiner, 'Pollution made COVID-19 worse. Now, lockdowns are clearing the air', *National Geographic*, 8 April 2020. Available from: www.nationalgeographic.com/science/2020/04/pollution-made-the-pandemic-worse-but-lockdowns-clean-the-sky/

When we talk about emerging environmental issues, we default to discussing climate change, centring our conversations around CO_2 emissions and air pollution. In the best case scenario, a 1.5° increase will trigger extreme temperatures, mass migration, crop shortages and political upheaval. For us to hit that goal, 'emissions in 2030 would have to be 55 per cent lower than they were in 2018' – a target many consider unlikely.[10] An increase of 2° is not a little worse; it is what scientists call the threshold for catastrophe. The seas will rise 10 centimetres or more and will displace millions, biodiversity loss will double, and several hundred million people will be thrust into poverty.[11] On the far end of the scenario spectrum, a 4 or 5° increase might drop the carrying capacity of the planet to one billion people or fewer.[12] There are eight billion of us now; what happens to those of us the planet can no longer sustain? Humanity might survive, but civilization will not.

What is left out of the above scenarios is that climate change is only part of the problem – one contributor to a complex disease. If we use COVID-19 as a metaphor, then rising temperatures, an inability to breathe and a condition that is more severe for some than others are analogous to climate change. It is entirely capable of being destructive on its own.

[10] Zoë Schlanger, 'The UN all but admits we will probably pass the 1.5°C point of no return', *Quartz*, 26 November 2019. Available from: qz.com/1755954/un-climate-report-says-warming-past-1-5c-is-likely/

[11] Megan Darby and Sara Stefanini, '37 things you need to know about 1.5C global warming', Climate Home News, 8 October 2018. Available from: www.climatechan-genews.com/2018/10/08/37-things-need-know-1-5c-global-warming/

[12] Kerry Sheridan, 'Earth risks tipping into "hothouse" state: study', Phys.org, 6 August 2018. Available from: phys.org/news/2018-08-earth-hothouse-state.html

The true scope of the problem emerges when you add other conditions into the mix. Similar to how pre-existing conditions fuelled COVID-19's impact on our bodies, there are other factors contributing to environmental degradation (i.e. the declining health of the overall system). These include ocean acidification, overconsumption, mounting waste, population explosion, deforestation and biodiversity loss, to name a few.[13] When we talk about climate change, we are talking about one part of the problem rather than how each part feeds into the others. The Earth's intricate balance of reinforcing relationships may be why we are hitting critical milestones like the loss of sea ice sooner than expected.[14] Nature is full of cascading effects in which a single change can trigger chaos across ecosystems. We do not understand those intricate relationships enough to know what outcomes our actions unwittingly bring about.

To make matters worse, the relationship between environmental degradation and infectious disease is well documented and researched. The worse our planetary conditions get, the more malaria, cholera and Lyme disease, among others, will flourish.[15] If one virus can bring humanity to its knees, imagine what a spectrum of diseases will do.

Beyond that lies the looming threat of environmental disaster. The Australian wildfires that ushered in 2020 inflicted an estimated AUD100 billion in immediate

[13]Janice Friedman, 'Environmental Degradation – What You Need To Know and Its Harmful Effects', Conservation Institute, 15 May 2018. Available from: www.conservationinstitute.org/environmental-degradation/

[14]Roger Harrabin, 'Faster pace of climate change is "scary", former chief scientist says', BBC News, 16 September 2019. Available from: www.bbc.com/news/science-environment-49689018

[15]'Climate change and human health – risks and responses. Summary', World Health Organization. Available from: www.who.int/globalchange/summary/en/index5.html

damage, not accounting for the wide range of long-term, intangible damage such as physical and mental health issues, domestic violence, unemployment and lost livestock.[16] The 2011 earthquake in Japan – which triggered a tsunami and nuclear incident – killed almost 16,000 people and caused $210 billion in economic damage.[17] It also decimated the global semiconductor supply chain, creating ripple effects for electronic manufacturers worldwide. As the environment degrades further, we can expect disasters on greater scales. Instead of fires, we will witness mega-fires. Instead of tsunamis, we can expect mega-tsunamis. Instead of hurricanes… well, you get the picture.

Once the disaster sets in, every aspect of society will turn towards managing the problem. Air, water and soil will all degrade. What individual, business, community or country can sustain itself without these fundamental resources? International relationships between allies will break down, similar to how countries and states competed for medical supplies. Global supply chains will collapse. Cities will sink. Widespread unrest will follow, paving the way for civil wars and dictatorships. There is a correlation between violence and a single standard deviation in weather.[18] In other words, the more volatile our environment, the more violent we

[16]Paul Reid and Richard Denniss, 'With costs approaching $100 billion, the fires are Australia's costliest natural disaster', The Conversation, 17 January 2020. Available from: theconversation.com/with-costs-approaching-100-billion-the-fires-are-australi-as-costliest-natural-disaster-129433

[17]Kimberly Amadeo, 'Japan's 2011 Earthquake, Tsunami and Nuclear Disaster', The Balance, 29 January 2020. Available from: www.thebalance.com/japan-s-2011-earthquake-tsunami-and-nuclear-disaster-3305662

[18]Bob O'Hara and GrrlScientist, 'Hot and bothered: Climate warming predicted to increase violent conflicts', Guardian. Available from: www.theguardian.com/science/grrlscientist/2013/aug/02/climate-change-global-warming-violence-conflict

become. With domestic and civil unrest, flourishing diseases, disasters and climate-induced illnesses, healthcare systems will be overburdened once more. The implications are so vast and far-reaching that we have barely begun to grasp how drastically our life will change. The changes brought on by COVID-19 pale in comparison to what environmental degradation will do.

In the context of our new world, some will react with altruism, empathy and sacrifice, while others will resort to greed, violence, ignorance and the like. When everyone is in constant crisis, there will be no one left to help. The idea that humanity will band together against a common enemy is a narrative that offers false hope; we have witnessed how a crisis like COVID-19 can divide us even further. We think the dystopias we see in movies are far-fetched futures, but we live in a world that descends into those patterns time and time again. Entropy is a law of the natural world and we are not the exception. It takes considerable effort and energy to maintain order.

Every wicked problem we have identified will be exacerbated beyond our comprehension if our planet declines further. The complex systems we have designed are tied to the planet, simply because it is our home, a shared resource without which we cannot survive. We also fail to comprehend how our lives will play out in decades, and the implications our present-day decisions have on our future selves. It is our children, grandchildren, and the generations that will come after who will pay for our actions.

Ultimately, there is no such thing as a stable economy without a stable planet. The economy is a subset of our social systems, which in turn are a subset of the environment. And yet we act as if it is the economy that sustains life on this planet, rather than simply our way of life as we know it. It is important to note here that we are not equally to blame, though we are all helping to maintain systems that are no longer serving us. Only 100 companies are responsible for 71 per cent of global emissions.[19] The top 10 per cent of wealthiest people consume approximately 20 times more energy than the bottom 10 per cent.[20] Addressing environmental degradation will require us to deconstruct our complex systems to identify the root issues driving them and reimagine what is possible, now and in the future, to bring about a world that can sustain all of us. The situation is dire but not lost.

Much like managing the COVID-19 crisis, significant collective effort will be required to mitigate environmental degradation. While it may be tempting to believe that the planet has recovered from a lack of human activity during the COVID-19 lockdown, all we managed was buying ourselves a little bit more time. For instance, as air pollution dropped, medical waste piled high.[21] One does not necessarily offset the other, but remember: the planet is a balanced system and we do not know what incident might tip the scales.

Our best course of action is the same strategy applied by New Zealand's Prime Minister Jacinda Ardern at the onset of COVID-19: behave as if you already have the virus. If we act as if environmental degradation is not only imminent, but

[19]Tess Riley, 'Just 100 companies responsible for 71 per cent of global emissions, study says', *Guardian*, 10 July 2017. Available from: www.theguardian.com/sustainable-business/2017/jul/10/100-fossil-fuel-companies-investors-responsible-71-global-emissions-cdp-study-climate-change

[20]Roger Harrabin, 'Climate change: The rich are to blame, international study finds', BBC News, 16 March 2020. Available from: www.bbc.com/news/business-51906530

[21]Farah Master and Yoyo Chow, 'Discarded coronavirus masks clutter Hong Kong's beaches, trails', Reuters, 12 March 2020. Available from: www.reuters.com/article/us-health-coronavirus-hongkong-environme/discarded-coronavirus-masks-clutter-hong-kongs-beaches-trails-idUSKBN20Z0PP

acknowledge that it is happening to us now, we can begin to reorient society towards sustainability. Acting as if the crisis is real might achieve more than mitigating the problem. It will take widespread change, compromise and effort, but the alternative (doing nothing or not enough) leads to mutually assured destruction.

Our persistent need for growth – a problematic narrative we have borrowed and misinterpreted from nature – is tied to strategies that demand extraction and exploitation. For example, GDP is a false measure of societal health and flourishing, and better reflects the manufacturing age we have left behind.[22] It no longer serves us, but it continues to drive policymaking towards short-term gain over long-term viability. Similarly, business is driven by a 'survival of the fittest' mentality, though nature demonstrates that co-operation, not competition (which requires more energy and resources for survival), is the preferred norm of species that flourish and the driver of evolution.[23] A harmonious society can benefit from doing the same and there are existing models that will allow us to move in that direction. Amsterdam has already committed to piloting Kate Raworth's Doughnut Economics approach to a post-COVID-19 world, in which the economy is balanced with the environment, signalling the shift to a more sustainable future.[24]

[22]David Pilling, '5 ways GDP gets it totally wrong as a measure of our success', World Economic Forum, 17 January 2018. Available from: www.weforum.org/agenda/2018/01/gdp-frog-matchbox-david-pilling-growth-delusion/
[23]'Cooperation, not struggle for survival, drives evolution, say researchers', ScienceDaily, 12 May 2016. Available from: www.sciencedaily.com/releases/2016/05/160512100708.htm
[24]Daniel Boffey, 'Amsterdam to embrace "doughnut" model to mend post-coronavirus economy', *Guardian*, 8 April 2020. Available from: www.theguardian.com/world/2020/apr/08/amsterdam-doughnut-model-mend-post-coronavirus-economy

As we move forward, we must make environmental sustainability a design consideration for every product, service, process, experience, policy, etc. that we create. In strategic foresight practice, long-term environmental sustainability is one of three criteria that serve as a minimum specification for future-proofing, without which your strategies and innovations may lack long-term viability.[25] Sustainability is not a hindrance or expense, rather it is a creative constraint that can spur a new era of innovation. Renewables, climate tech and a plethora of other environmentally sound products, services and solutions are available for scale if only we would invest in them (many major investment funds are moving in that direction).[26] We already have everything we need to bring about a flourishing world. What we lack is a willingness to let go of our entrenched systems of power – the few we preserve at the expense of the many and the generations yet to come. For instance, while countries like South Korea embraced the EU's Green Deal during the COVID-19 crisis, the United States chose to bail out fossil fuels in a bid to preserve a dying industry that threatens to take us all down with it.[27,28]

---

[25]Leah Zaidi, 'The only three trends that matter: A minimum specification for future-proofing', *Journal of Futures Studies*. Available from: jfsdigital.org/the-only-three-trends-that-matter-a-minimum-specification-for-future-proofing/

[26]Robert G. Eccles and Svetlana Klimenko, 'The Investor Revolution', *Harvard Business Review*, May–June 2019 Issue. Available from: hbr.org/2019/05/the-investor-revolution

[27]David Vetter, 'South Korea Embraces EU-Style Green Deal For COVID-19 Recovery', Forbes, 16 April 2020. Available from: www.forbes.com/sites/davidrvetter/2020/04/16/south-korea-embraces-eu-style-green-deal-for-covid-19-recovery/#-5f6a9e855611

[28]David Roberts, 'Coronavirus stimulus money will be wasted on fossil fuels', *Vox*, 20 April 2020. Available from: www.vox.com/2020/4/20/21224659/coronavirus-stimulus-money-oil-prices-fossil-fuels-bailout

Policy will need to play a significant role, but organizations can help implement powerful changes in the meantime. The companies that survive the longest are those that are able to adapt to the shifting needs of the ecosystems they inhabit. Organizations that have survived more than a hundred years have actively shaped society by looking 20 to 30 years ahead, and responding to the needs of tomorrow.[29] They do not wait for a crisis to react, especially not when the pressure to act is increasing. A survey of 1,168 CFOs revealed that despite stakeholder demands to take comprehensive action, 'a thorough understanding of climate risks is rare' and 'few companies have a governance and steering mechanism in place to develop and implement comprehensive climate strategies'.[30] Public-private co-operation and the integration of relevant experts into the upper tiers of organizations might help facilitate the process.

If nothing else, smart organizations understand the importance of aligning themselves with the values of younger generations who will increasingly demand greater action. With global shutdowns forcing us to change our lifestyles and re-evaluate our priorities, those value shifts may happen faster than we expected. In the UK, only 9 per cent of Britons wanted life to go back to normal after weeks of experiencing

[29]Alex Hill, Liz Mellon and Jules Goddard, 'How Winning Organizations Last 100 Years', *Harvard Business Review*, 27 September 2018. Available from: hbr.org/2018/09/how-winning-organizations-last-100-years

[30]Michela Coppola, Thomas Krick, Julian Blomhke, 'Feeling the heat? Companies are under pressure on climate change and need to do more', *Deloitte*, 12 December 2019. Available from: www2.deloitte.com/us/en/insights/topics/strategy/impact-and-opportunities-of-climate-change-on-business.html

'cleaner air, more wildlife and stronger communities'.[31] Change is taking root.

As with COVID-19, environmental degradation places us in a prisoner's dilemma scenario: acting with self-interest when facing a collective crisis leaves us all worse off. Though COVID-19 is a crisis, it is also an opportunity to avert greater disaster. We have witnessed the power of early intervention and disciplined collective action – the power we wield through simple acts such as staying home, power that can be put to better use. We have seen the benefits of slowing down our economy, as well as the challenges that come with lack of preparedness for disruptive change. If we fail to learn from this crisis, we will doom ourselves to repeat it – and next time, we may not recover. Our planet is demanding respect. The only way to ensure a sustainable future for humanity is to make it a present-day reality.

[31]Lucia Binding, 'Coronavirus: Only 9 per cent of Britons want life to return to "normal" once lockdown is over', Sky News, 17 April 2020. Available from: news. sky.com/story/coronavirus-only-9-of-britons-want-life-to-return-to-normal-once-lockdown-is-over-11974459

3

Information Overload

By Manish Bahl, leading futurist, keynote speaker and Associate Vice President of Cognizant's Center for the Future of Work

Can we survive on the information we truly need to make decisions rather than harvesting data on everything, all the time? Why do we need to be bombarded with data-derived choice, and will this ultimately lead to the dumbing down of society? What happens to the generation that does not have to think for itself about anything? What happens when our shrinking attention spans and omniscient 'spatial web' connections mean we forget how and why to read and write? The future problem for individuals and organizations is too much, not too little information. In a world that is constantly collecting, tracking, and sharing data, how do you distil what is important and what is just a distraction? And how can we claw back the stillness and space we need?

Dear Future Generations,

It's not your fault. This world you're living in, where your online reputation and social media score determines every aspect of your life, from your relationships to your career; where words like 'instinct', 'intuition' and 'gut feeling' no longer have any meaning; where humanity is measured in bits and bytes: it's all on us – your previous generations. How did it come to this? What did we do to leave you this legacy? We made some mistakes. Let me explain.

It wasn't always this way. People were once intelligent and self-reliant. They had common sense, loved to interact with each other in person, and could think logically. They took decisions based on context, in real time. But things changed. We started to move more and more of ourselves online when we saw that 'virtual' life could be so much more interesting than real life. Every click, purchase, swipe, thumbs up or thumbs down – the digital footprints we left behind started to feel exciting, addictive, and the more we left, the more we made. And that's when things started to get really interesting; as digital platforms began to give a new meaning to our online presence. We trusted Netflix for movies, Amazon for books, Facebook for friendships, and Google for information – *Wow, this movie recommendation platform knows my taste better than my spouse! I've never heard of this author, but she sounds amazing!* And so on. We started to depend more on digital platforms for information, and custom, curated experiences to get those 'Aha!' moments of magic. It almost felt like these platforms could read our minds as they anticipated and fulfilled information we might not have ever found by ourselves. We took decisions based on online ratings and reviews: which restaurant to dine in, which pair of jeans to buy, what music to listen to.

We became so deeply immersed in this vastly connected world that our virtual lives started to reflect our real lives – but *better*. We could edit our real life before sharing it with the world: add filters to our photos, airbrush our blemishes, delete what we didn't want anyone to see and post only what made us feel good about ourselves. From our food to our faces, from our pets to our holidays, we could subtly change the narrative of our day-to-day lives. Human conversations were slowly replaced with 'updates' and 'likes'. Fewer 'likes' on our posts meant friends and family were losing interest, and our self-worth took a nosedive. Without those human conversations to fall back on, we turned instead to smart devices for interaction and guidance: personal voice assistants bought our groceries, refrigerators bought our milk, and our toothbrushes booked dental appointments for us. Life became so comfortable and smooth in its interconnectedness.

We had unimaginable amounts of information at our fingertips 24/7, and it was *compelling*. We came to think of ourselves as super-smart and intelligent. We could find out anything, *know* anything, do anything, without the hassle of having to study. What was not to love? But you know how this story ends, of course. Our over-reliance on information and data-derived choices gradually began to bite back. For our previous generations, information was harder to come by: people had to visit a library, or look through an encyclopaedia, but for us, information became abundant. Overabundant. And the more we had, the more we needed. Our greed for information began to kill off our need to learn, and ultimately – ironically – led to the dumbing down of our society. We became more interested in knowing the name of a new royal baby than whether there really was a serious issue with climate change. We over-relied on GPS to get to well-known landmarks, even though we'd lived in the same city all our lives. We became so addicted to information that the urge to check our smartphone at 3 a.m. to keep up with what was happening in the world stopped us from getting a good night's sleep. We became so afraid of missing out on one tiny, possibly critical piece of knowledge that we never fully disconnected. We started checking our phones more than 60 times a day. All this information, all the time, yet still we struggled with fundamental questions: Do we need this much data? What are we doing with all the data? What's our purpose? And what's the meaning of data-driven life?

Not everyone was caught up in and sold on this constant data cycle. Many mindful experts warned us of the downside to our overdependence on data-driven thinking. Too much information, they cautioned, was disconnecting humans from humanity. Did we pay their warnings any heed? In reading this letter, this warning of my own, you know of course that we didn't. Where they saw risk, we saw only benefits. We didn't want to be left behind, or miss out. We were so constantly in receipt of notifications from our digital devices that any absence of signal for more than a few minutes made us anxious, irritable and moody. And here's where the consequences of our new lifestyle began to show themselves. Attention deficit disorder became rampant. The human attention span had been decreasing for us by 88 per cent every year, and as I write this it now stands at just eight seconds.[32] Today, 45 per cent of human behaviour centres on unthinking tasks. Our dependency on the virtual world made us less observant, blinkered, almost, and we lost touch with noticing what we're doing, or thinking, or where we were going.

[32]Jia Wertz, 'The Number One Thing Marketers Need to Know to Increase On-line Sales', Forbes, 31 August 2019. Available from: www.forbes.com/sites/jiawertz/2019/08/31/the-number-one-thing-marketers-need-to-know-to-increase-online-sales/#19e99e817fed

As we lived more and more of our life online, we began to lose all concepts of emotional connection; we were continually transformed into bits and bytes based on our virtual actions rather than our biological ones, causing stress, anxiety, depression and sleeplessness. What would happen to us when our shrinking attention spans and omniscient 'spatial web' connections meant we forgot how to read and write? What if we forgot why we ever learned to read and write in the first place? Or if intelligent machines could read and write better than us? I can't believe how ignorant we became, and all by choice.

With so much information coming at us from new sources, and at such high speeds, it was only ever a matter of time before this information we gorged ourselves on became corrupted. With no army of editors checking encyclopaedia entries, no meticulous lawyers fact-checking documents before they're posted, fake news and fake information began to become widespread. Elections were influenced, democracy and society threatened. We started to drown in the sea of information that kept us distracted from our real-world problems. It became almost impossible to recognize the truth any more. To paraphrase Mark Twain, 'lies run much faster than the truth'. This still holds true for my time; I can only hope the same can't be said of yours. Many experts claimed we needed stricter regulations to control information, or even enforce internet curfews, but the horrifying truth was that regulations could never keep pace with technological advancements. We never had a hope of controlling the fake information.

With the availability of so much information being seen as culpable in the raising of an antisocial generation, you could be forgiven for wondering if there's anything good I can say about it. The truth, as we understood it, is that technology undeniably improved our society overall. Real-time data helped us make education, healthcare, government and many other industries in our times truly smart.

The worst pandemic of my time, triggered by the COVID-19 virus, made each of us realize how much of a blessing technology is in our lives. The virus forced us, as a society, to completely change everything that constituted our normal lives. We became confined to our homes in an attempt to save ourselves, our families and our neighbours from the horrors of the virus. Suddenly, technology became the only thing keeping us connected during our enforced social isolation. We Skyped our parents instead of visiting them; we went to our laptops and opened Zoom instead of going to the office. Moving even more of our lives online kept us connected, kept us working, and kept us safe. We came to fully understand, perhaps for the first time, how much we needed to embrace advanced technologies and data-driven thinking to treat and defeat both the current virus and future pandemics. Maybe this was the time we should have asked ourselves what type of world we wanted to leave behind for future generations. A completely tech-oriented society, or a human-oriented, tech-enabled society? But we had a few too many things on our mind at the time.

It can often take a life-changing event to put things in perspective. To truly drive change. After the terrorist attack on the World Trade Center in the US in 2001, the flying experience was irrevocably changed overnight. Massive security infrastructure was implemented to ensure such an attack could never happen again. With this in mind, will it take a robot Armageddon now to shake us deeply enough to realize that we have surrendered ourselves too completely to intelligent machines? If such an event were to happen, would we still have time to overcome our mistakes, or would it be too late for us? What should we have done? Should we have powered down our digital lives completely, and gone back to the old days of dusty libraries and instantly out-of-date encyclopaedias? What would *you* have done, in our time?

We, as humans, across all generations, have the opportunity to determine our future. Yet with great power comes great responsibility. Extraordinary times, no matter which generation you're from, require extraordinary measures. Our generation should have stepped up and dealt with the issue head-on. I wish our governments had defined and implemented a 'healthy information diet' for everyone to follow. Every citizen could have had an information consumption dashboard, showing how much information they needed to survive each day. Just like too much unhealthy food makes us ill, too much information makes us sick, mentally. If we had made healthy information consumption a new attribute for education, healthcare, employment, it would have made a difference. This change in mindset would have required concentrated efforts from individuals, companies, governments, and our overall society. Our responsibility was to create a world we would want to live in. Did we meet that responsibility? You'll be better able to answer that than me. I am sorry we didn't do enough.

In my time, we're now fast approaching a future of artificial intelligence, putting even more trust in machines. We're not far from the point when machines will begin to make our life decisions for us, fundamentally calling our identity as independent humans into question. We are now putting all our hopes on the shoulders of your generation. I hope you can learn from our mistakes, and bring about a radical change in the way we consume information. Ultimately, I hope you can make the world more *human* again.

Yours,
Relentlessly Optimistic for a Better Future

4

In Defence of Imperfect Information

By Bronwyn Williams, futurist, economist and trend analyst

All the world's a stage, yet what happens when there is no more 'backstage'? On the surveillance state and having nowhere to hide (from creditors, taxmen, states and corporations), and conversely, on the benefits of transparency. Do we really want to live in for-profit private city-states? Does your government really need to know who you are sleeping with? Is perfect information a worthy goal? And what about businesses? Do companies have a right to know their competitors' secrets? What about the secrets of their consumers – or employees? And where does one draw the line? This essay looks at the trade-offs between privacy, security and costs, and calls for more informed consent when it comes to the trade-offs between trading our privacy for freedom, or free stuff.

I don't know about you, but I love secrets. I am a defender of imperfect information and an advocate for the right to privacy.

Why be concerned about privacy if you have nothing to hide? If you have committed no crimes and have lived a blameless life with nothing to be ashamed of, you should theoretically have no need for secrets at all.

Or perhaps you've given up on the practicality of privacy. Perhaps you believe that technology has rendered privacy impossible or even *undesirable* from a social good perspective.

Perhaps you simply believe that privacy is unimportant.

I, however, believe all those views are wrong. I believe privacy is a right worth protecting, for both personal and professional reasons.

SECRETS AND LIES

We all have secrets. I know I certainly do.

We all have things that we don't want anyone else to know. Things like: how much money we have (or don't). A closely guarded family recipe. The embarrassing guilty pleasure we take in listening to cheesy 90s pop music. How much time we spend scrolling through social media feeds. Who we are (really) in love with. The affair we had at a particularly vulnerable time in our marriage. The distressing diagnosis we just received from our doctor. Where we buried the bodies (figuratively speaking, of course).

And the truth is, without some secrets, without a private inner life, we lose our sense of self. The boundaries between our inner and outer lives are in many ways what really make us individuals in the first place. As such, privacy is a key part of freedom and free will.

More so, privacy is a right that should be enjoyed equally by all. Privacy should not be a luxury reserved only for those rich enough to reside behind high walls and build bunkers out of sight of the all-seeing satellites that spy on us from above. Privacy, the right to withhold information and the right to be forgotten are not trinkets or status symbols, they are a requirement for human flourishing.

RIGHT TO BE FORGOTTEN

Regarding the right to be forgotten, we should be able to walk into our futures without the mistakes of our past dictating our access to opportunity. That's not to say that we should not pay for our crimes or take responsibility for our sins, but rather that once our debt to society is paid, once we have done our time, we should be afforded the luxury of a clean slate and the chance to reinvent ourselves on our own terms. After all, who among us is not embarrassed by a former action in our distant history we would never dream of repeating?

Increasingly, though, our indelible digital footprints follow us around throughout our lives. We have no privacy from our past. This means we are unable to reinvent ourselves and we are unable to forgive and forget the transgressions of those around us.

Does a young female politician deserve to have her future career destroyed because of a topless photograph taken when she was a teenager? Does a 60-year-old man deserve to have the unwise words he wrote in jest in his youth on his social media profile follow him to the grave?

No. Perhaps we should agree that our personal past is best preserved with imperfect information. Some things are best forgotten, or at least best not exposed to the general public.

SOCIAL COOLING

Similarly, the trend towards perfect information is also pushing us towards social cooling. Social cooling refers to self-censorship in exchange for social acceptance. This global social cooling is the cumulative long-term negative effect of living in the quantified reputation economy without the right to be forgotten – where our every action, thought, tweet and like is surveilled, recorded, scrutinized and used to rank our place in society.

With every device we connect to our bodies, with every camera we install to watch our public (and, increasingly, private) spaces, we give up more of the shadows and contours that make us who we are. We behave – indeed even think – differently when we know we are being watched, nudged to the lowest common acceptable denominator. In a society where no one is prepared to step out of line, the cost of dissenting from the majority grows exponentially.

If there is nowhere to escape from the big data dragnet and our lives are always under scrutiny, from smartwatches, city street cameras and live-streaming social media services, if we are always on stage, on view, being judged and there is no more backstage or offstage, where will any of us feel safe to be ourselves? A world where everyone is always watching everyone else for cues on how to behave and what opinions to hold is a world where innovation slows and eventually stops. A world in which mistakes are never forgotten is not a world where risk-taking and creativity are encouraged. The pervasive culture of conformity stifles creativity and innovation as much as it does free speech – if no one is prepared to take a chance on a new idea that might end in failure or ridicule, the long-term effect is to 'cool down' society's growth and development.

This point alone should be of concern to anyone interested in a future that is more prosperous than the present.

We need to resist the inertia of social cooling. As we are monitored and nudged into complacency by omniscient technology monitoring a society that never forgets or forgives, we need to fight for the right to be imperfect, make mistakes, take chances and stand out. This lack of privacy is not good for both the individual and for society at large.

THE GREATER 'GOOD'

Of course, one of the big arguments against privacy is that a lack of privacy is for the greater good. We are encouraged to accept, nay even welcome, ubiquitous street level and online surveillance as a method of both deterring and catching criminals. In many countries, citizens are encouraged to submit to cell phone location and contact tracing to monitor and prevent the spread of contagious disease. We are encouraged to share our likes, opinions and purchase history with advertisers and businesses in exchange for more targeted offers tailored to unearthing and meeting our unique needs and desires. We are expected to share our grocery lists, our exercise habits, our step counts and even (as is likely in the not too distant future) our DNA with our insurers and banks in exchange for gentle nudges and rewards for good behaviour.

This sounds all well and good at first; however, when we take the time to consider the deeper exchange at play, privacy sacrificed for the greater good might not be so benign after all.

Think about it. Asking innocent citizens to give up their privacy and submit to state surveillance and location tracking through devices that are to all intents and purposes tantamount to ankle monitors in their phones is essentially assuming all citizens are guilty until proven innocent. Of course crime rates would decrease if you put your entire population under constant surveillance. However, is the security of the resulting gilded cage worth the price paid? Should the majority of innocent souls have to pay for the sins of the few with their dignity? Perhaps not.

Or what about the implicit inequality present in any commercial trade of personal data or privacy in exchange for access to goods or services? It is obvious that the poorer and more disadvantaged among us would be under more pressure to give up their secrets and themselves in exchange for a living than would the rich; and for a lower price too. A poor man could be persuaded to submit to state surveillance and strict behavioural rules in exchange for a universal basic income – or even for a discount on a data bill. A rich man, however, can afford to hold on to his secrets and reject surveillance as a means to survival.

Indeed, there are marginal returns to wholesale voyeurism.

Because although public health, safety, security and productivity are good and reasonable goals, the increasing trade-off with our personal privacy and freedoms results in ever-diminishing, marginal returns of those same common goods in exchange for an ever-greater price.

For every drop of our real selves, our secrets and our freedoms that we sacrifice on the altar of the greater good, we get less and less individual security in return.

Ultimately, the resulting greater good is not all that good, or all that great, if it comes at the cost of punishing the innocent along with the guilty.

ADVERSE SELECTION

Now, even if sacrificing one's privacy to the greater or individual good is in some way justifiable from a social justice perspective (who could argue against saving a life at almost any price?), there is still the commercial question of imperfect information to consider.

Adverse selection refers to when one side of a trade has access to materially significant information hidden from the other side of the trade that, if known to both parties, would have affected the price and terms of the deal. For example, a second-hand car sales person who knowingly sells an unsuspecting buyer a 'lemon' (that is, a defective vehicle), or a smoker taking out medical insurance without informing their insurer of their risky habit. Theoretically, perfect information solves this problem. If both sides of a trade have access to all the information regarding the quality and the risk of the trade, adverse selection should no longer apply. This is superficially a good argument against privacy, particularly when it comes to withholding health and habit information from insurers and states (where states are responsible for funding medical bills).

However, when you consider the problem from a wider perspective, we find that all that has really changed from an insurance perspective is that adverse selection has shifted from the buy side of the market to the sell side of the market. Consider a case where an insurer insists on a DNA test to determine the likelihood of a particular individual developing a genetically linked disease. This access to perfect information makes sense from the insurer's perspective, as the invasion of the client's privacy and personal bio data allows the insurer to make a better risk analysis and set more perfect premium prices. However, this sort of testing also means that the insurer who has access to the test results and to the actuarial models that determine the risk profile of the prospective client also has a perverse incentive to withhold that same risk profile from that same prospective client. The prospective client would not have access to the same analytical tools and tests as the insurer.

Now, we could take this example further and suggest that it should become law that both the buy and sell side of such a trade be forced to disclose all their relevant information. We could suggest that insurance clients should be obligated to share their bio data, their diet, their health habits and their movements with their insurers. We could mandate trackers in our bodies, in our fridges and in our cars to ensure the information provided to our insurers is perfect. At the same time, we could mandate that insurance companies share their workings with their clients and the public at large. We could insist that DNA test results and actuarial models are completely transparent. But then, as we look ahead to a world where truly perfect information becomes possible, we run into another problem. If both sides of the market have access to perfect information, as that source data becomes more and more complete, and those prediction models become more and more accurate, we find ourselves painted into a corner. If insurers and their clients have access to practically perfect information, why should anyone purchase such an insurance policy at all? As the price of insurance premiums approaches the actual cost of the risk with increased accuracy, the incentive to take out insurance at all approaches zero…

Yes, this is an extreme hypothetical example, but the principle of how reducing uncertainty reduces profitability is still a useful thought exercise, highlighting the intrinsic commercial value of privacy.

MARGIN IS IN THE MYSTERY

Then we come to competition.

There is an old business adage that says that the *margin is in the mystery*. This is sage advice. When it comes to competitive advantage, commercial secrets – privacy – is where profitability lies. Whether you are a consultant selling processes and procedures, or you are a sugary drinks company selling a beverage made to a secret recipe or patented formula, the mystery makes the margin.

Imagine that all companies were forced to expose their secrets. Imagine that each firm was forced to disclose the salaries they paid to each and every staff member. Imagine that every company was forced to disclose the exact details of their product costings, formulas, supply chain contacts, deal terms, strategic plans, boardroom minutes, markups and margins to the general public (and their competition). Imagine how much value would be removed from the marketplace, along with the mystery.

So much of success lies in the secret source.

THE CONSENSUS

It is not impossible to imagine a future where many of the privacy erosions listed above come to pass. A world where transparency is the norm and all individual secrets and mysteries – be they personal, professional or commercial – are sacrificed for the greater good.

But now cast your mind even further forward to a world where human minds become connected to the connected cloud, and neurological implants can both *receive and transmit* information to the Internet. In other words, a world where perfect information is ubiquitous and inescapable. In this super-connected future, there would be nowhere to hide any secrets, not even within the privacy of your own thoughts. In such a world, even thinking out of line would be close to impossible, as you would be constantly connected and constantly exposed to the meta-consensus of the entirety of the Internet of People. There would be no individuality, and no escape from the omniscient all.

Yes, such a vision does appear to be highly speculative. However, neuroscientists and technologists working on 'Brainternet' projects believe that such a fantastic internet of all the people is indeed possible. Some even believe it is desirable to build such a world of perfect information; they believe that if we could all know and understand each other's thoughts and innermost secrets, world conflict would cease and we could finally achieve global harmony – true *consensus*.

But at what cost?

THERE IS MAGIC IN THE MYSTERY

I'll leave you to decide if you find such a logical eventual conclusion to the eradication of individuality and privacy to be a utopia or a dystopia.

That said, I hope that this essay has at least enabled you to understand the personal and economic value of a little secrecy in the present world we live in.

Privacy is not dead, but it is on life support. I for one would like to see it pull through. And not just for those rich enough to pay for the privilege either.

After all, we dance differently when no one is looking. We dream differently when no one is listening in.

There is magic as well as margin in the mystery.

PART TWO

A New World Requires New Thinking

How much do you value yourself?

How much do you value your present self compared to your future self?

How much do you value your contemporaries' lives compared to the lives of future generations?

When it comes to the allocation of resources, most of us are biased towards the present. We discount the future and overvalue the present. This is not entirely unreasonable. Life is finite. We have no guarantees that we will even have a future at all. Still, if we are sensible, we will aim to, as economists say, 'smooth' our consumption (that is, enjoyment of life) as much as possible over our entire expected lifespan. For most of us, that lifespan will be a good 70–90 years. This means that borrowing – that is, spending – some of our expected future income (assuming we expect our future income to be more than our present income) today makes good sense. As such, most of us borrow money when we are young to invest in education, housing, businesses and other assets, betting that the future value of the asset will be worth more than the future value of the debt we are taking on. This strategy makes sense, as long as we eventually earn back what we have pre-spent. There is, after all, no such thing as a free lunch – only debate over who pays the bill and when.

The question, however, is how much of our future happiness, wealth and enjoyment we are prepared to sacrifice on the altar of now. And how much of the lives of others, present and future, we are prepared to sacrifice to improve our own present.

What is the future worth to you? – will you discount it, or will you invest in it?

Of course, the same line of thinking applies not just to individuals but to society as a whole, working backwards from future protopia to present reality.

In this section, our authors explore the potential shape of a *new world* and present their thoughts on the trade-offs, constraints, incentives and choices that will shape the future geopolitical and economic landscape.

After reading this section, we recommend you reflect on the consequences of your own individual and organizational choices, and decide what sort of game it is that you are really playing. Are you playing the long game or the short game? Are you engaged in extracting value, or in creating value? Are you building a legacy, or leaving a pile of debt or (literal or figurative) mess behind for someone else – be that another nation or another generation – to clean up?

5

The Revolution in Tech Requires a Revolution in Policy

By Chris Yiu, Executive Director of the Technology and Public Policy team at the Tony Blair Institute for Global Change

As old empires collapse under their own weight, and new powers arise, we must not forget that the new geopolitical fault lines emerging are virtual rather than geographic. Those who control the narrative control the future; and those who control the flows of information – that is, today, our technological infrastructure and networks – control the narrative. This essay looks at policy from a futurist's lens, analysing how we can protect both our nations and our individual identities as the new (virtual) world emerges.

In politics and at the centre of government, it is easy to underestimate the pace and scale of change in the wider world. This is a profound mistake.

The technological revolution we are living through in the early 21st century is the modern-day equivalent of the 19th-century Industrial Revolution. The defining technologies of our time – computer power, bandwidth and storage on tap, machine learning, advanced biotechnology – are changing the economy to dramatic effect, just as steam power, mechanized textile production and machine tools did in their day.

But the impact of the first Industrial Revolution wasn't just felt by businesses and workers. The ripple effects of new technologies changed everything around them. Over the century that followed, as the nature of work and wealth generation moved with new technologies, the structure of communities changed; political movements and parties shifted and evolved. The very nature of government and the welfare state underwent a fundamental alteration to respond to and in time represent the new and varied coalitions emerging in industrial society.

Now, just as then, the revolution in technology presages a wider revolution in our economy and society – and demands that government and politics change in order to remain relevant. This time, though, the pace of change is an order of magnitude faster.

In the Industrial Revolution of the 19th century, the half-life of skills was around 50 years and the knock-on effects on government and political institutions took perhaps 100 years to fully work through.

In the technological revolution of the 21st century, the half-life of skills is more like five years. If change really is happening ten times faster than before, our institutions need to be able to completely reinvent themselves on a timescale more like a decade than a century. But around the world, the thing that many governments do best is seek to maintain the status quo.

As we survey everything that has happened in the world in recent years, it is clear that the industrial-era institutions that house the world's policy and political infrastructure are structurally mismatched for the new challenges and opportunities ahead of us.

The revolution in technology therefore demands nothing less than a complete revolution in policymaking, politics and the business of government.

In the context of this debate, there are three big and interrelated trends that cut across policy, business, technology and society. The first is the seismic shift in the information environment resulting from widespread access to the Internet. The second is the emergence of new superpowers based on private technology. And the third is the way widespread access to advanced technology is empowering small groups to innovate faster than incumbent organizations.

THE EXPLODED INFORMATION SPHERE

The information environment that people, businesses and governments operate in has undergone a radical and irreversible transformation over the past few decades.

Before the arrival of the Internet and social media, the information environment was governed by gatekeepers born of the institutions of the industrial era: newspaper editors, broadcasters, business leaders, government officials and political parties. As citizens, we still had choice about the sources of information we would consume – but within carefully demarcated limits, and with limited access to opportunities to challenge the prevailing narrative.

The arrival of the Internet, the World Wide Web and then social media completely upended the information sphere.

Not only do we have effectively unlimited access to alternative points of view, we have also made the transition to a world where anyone and everyone is a content creator as well as a content consumer.

Much has been written about the fallout from these developments, from the impact on the fourth estate and public interest journalism through to the implications for privacy, copyright and filter bubbles. For our discussion, the most relevant and direct impact of the information revolution is the way that it has collapsed the distance between the public and those in positions of authority.

Before this shift, control of the public narrative went hand in hand with control of the direction of public policy and political debate. Of course governments came and went, and some achieved more than others. But the trajectory of policy was one of gradual evolution, punctuated by the occasional generational shift or scandal.

In the exploded information sphere of the 21st century, there is no possibility of a dominant narrative. Online and on social media, the institutions that held so much weight in the industrial era compete with an effectively infinite array of alternative voices. All have equal access to the technology for mass communication, and attention flows not towards those in positions of seniority but rather towards those who are prepared to tell people what they want to hear.

As the former CIA analyst Martin Gurri observes, the result is nothing short of a crisis of authority.[33]

This has a direct bearing on policymaking because it strikes at the very heart of the approach that has dominated politics

[33]Martin Gurri, *The Revolt of The Public and the Crisis of Authority in the New Millennium* (California Stripe Press, San Francisco, 2018)

and government since the industrial era. Every public policy decision creates losers as well as winners; the difference now is that those on the losing side have direct access to the means to voice their dissent. Similarly, every public policy decision embodies a huge amount of detail and complexity that typically remained out of public focus unless someone dedicated significant resources to investigating it. In the modern information environment, everyone is empowered to expose problems and inconsistencies, and to achieve this in close to real time.

As leaders around the world are discovering, trying to press ahead against these forces is already hard, and getting harder by the day. The only way out of paralysis is a completely different approach to how policy is conceived and developed.

The same tools that have empowered the public versus traditional institutions also give us the potential to launch new sorts of policy dialogue: to share the evidence informing the debate, to deliberate together and flush out difficult trade-offs, and to track the impact of new measures transparently and in granular detail.

Making this happen is as much about culture and leadership as it is about the specific tools and technologies that are being deployed around the world. This is closely connected to the most effective ways to configure organizations for the future. We will return to this theme at the end of this chapter, but first we need to turn to our second big trend: the rising power of tech companies.

NEW SOURCES OF POWER

The great power conflicts of the industrial era were anchored in nation states, whether in conflict or competing in the marketplace of the global economy. Of course, through the years there have been individuals, organizations and companies that have accumulated significant wealth and achieved great influence. But the ultimate source of power in society has been political: only governments write laws, negotiate treaties and have a monopoly over the use of force.

The revolution in technology has completely altered the locus of power. In particular, the power of large technology companies has arguably reached parity with – or in some domains, surpassed – that of governments and nation states.

As with the story of the information revolution, the ascent of the big tech companies has been rehearsed many times. In fact, the two are intimately connected – some of the biggest tech companies are deeply intertwined with the information environment, both creating the technologies that facilitate it and responding to the new dynamics it has created.

What is often missed, however, is that modern technology makes these companies fundamentally different to those born in the industrial age. The cost structure of internet businesses is often characterized by massive fixed costs and effectively zero marginal costs for production, distribution and transactions. The net result is consistent with the world we see around us: businesses are subject to a powerful incentive to scale up to as big a user base as possible, and many markets are winner-takes-all (or winner-takes-most) even at a regional or global scale.

But when the market capitalization of a handful of companies exceeds that of so many others, and when the number of users for global technology platforms runs into the hundreds of millions or even billions, then it is impossible for this not to affect the balance of power.

And so in some respects we are all citizens of the Internet economy as well as citizens of our countries and cities. Those in charge of the tech platforms may not write laws in the traditional sense, but they set the terms and conditions of service, they determine the community standards that govern acceptable behaviour, and they enforce the rules to the point of sanctioning or removing users who break the rules.

The top-down regulation and institutions of the 20th century are a poor fit for this new reality. And nor can those in positions of political power rely on it to force compliance with their world view (just ask one of the countless number who have tried and failed and, as per the exploded information environment, often come out the other side looking somewhat foolish).

The great temptation for those in positions of political power is to seek to tear down the new power bases being built up around technology. But while this may sometimes be politically expedient, it's not a sustainable position to hold. Technology platforms inevitably tend towards scale, and they do this by providing a service that most people value. Of course, there have been many mistakes made along the way, and those on the wrong side of disruption have not always fared well. But it would be a mistake to frame this as a confrontation.

What is required instead is a revolution in our approach to regulating the businesses that are in the vanguard of change in the 21st century. Perhaps in time more governments will have technical expertise and speed of operation on a par with the big tech companies. But the first step is to understand their culture, business strategy and incentives in order to formulate a radically different approach to how we engage with them.

Ultimately, the challenge is that the biggest technology companies in the world – both those in the United States and their peers and competitors in China – wield enormous power, but often do so clumsily and without a level of legitimacy to match their scale and reach. Addressing this requires some significant soul-searching for all of us: about the values we want to govern a world that is increasingly shifting online, and where national boundaries are a relic of a bygone era.

It also demands a faster, more agile and responsive approach to policymaking. The shift away from big, hierarchical organizations is our third and final trend to explore.

NETWORKS NOT HIERARCHIES

The great institutions of the industrial age – those increasingly exposed by an exploded information sphere and challenged by new sources of power – are all built around industrial age models of organization. This is a shape that is familiar to many of us: hierarchy, bureaucracy, the great pyramid where decisions are centralized and information is cascaded from top to bottom.

This is not how things work on the frontiers of the technological revolution.

The infrastructure of the 20th century was roads and railways, power, telecommunications and government administration. Bricks and mortar organizations built on physical infrastructure typically required significant capital expenditures to get up and running and relied on centralized decision-making in order to co-ordinate different activities towards a common goal.

The infrastructure of the 21st century is digital: new generations of low-latency, high-bandwidth mobile data networks and, just as importantly, the data and software layers that underpin so much of modern life. The organizations born on the Internet typically require minimal capital expenditures to get up and running, consuming everything they need as a service that scales in tandem with their operations. And because modern technology can eliminate so much of the friction within organizations, it becomes much easier for different parts to innovate and experiment without coming adrift from the whole.

Hence, among some of the most interesting organizations and businesses on the forefront of the technological revolution, we are starting to see fascinating variety in organizational structures, talent pools and ways of working. Hierarchies are getting flatter, and in some cases are superseded entirely by self-organizing units (see, for example, Spotify's squads, tribes, guilds and alliances). Multidisciplinary teams are showing that they can outperform traditional specialized alternatives, with engineers and product managers working alongside designers and operations colleagues.

Even the workplace itself is changing, with many organizations now designing to prioritize collaboration and spontaneity or embracing a shift to remote working. Among the tech companies where these trends are the furthest ahead, many are now expecting a significant proportion of their staff to work at least partly from home – increasing flexibility and giving people back the time they would otherwise have spent on a commute. Automattic, the company behind WordPress.com, famously has an entirely distributed organization with no HQ.

These changes are more than superficial – they reflect a deep-seated shift towards a way of working that prioritizes knowledge sharing and collaboration, that is open rather than closed, and that is reflected in the culture and ambition of the people involved.

The worlds of policy and politics are often among the last to embrace these sorts of changes. But there are glimmers of a new approach taking hold, whether it is in the UK's award-winning Government Digital Service, the civic participation and digital democracy drive in Taiwan, or the great strides being made to forge a new path at Code for America.

Even now, in the foothills of the technological revolution, it is clear that talent and human capital will be the most precious commodity that any organization – public or private – will seek to access and accumulate in the years ahead. The best people will gravitate to the places where they can take technology and freedom and convert them into impact.

The next great wave of change is upon us, and those people and institutions occupying the fields of policymaking, politics and government are not and will not be immune from its effects. If we freeze in its wake and let it wash over us, we risk being marooned in a sea of decline. But if we ride it with courage and intelligence, then a bright future awaits.

6

Casualties of War

By Kristina Libby, Chief Science Officer at Hypergiant

Misinformation, disinformation, propaganda or fake news, call it what you will: the new centre of global conflict is around claiming territory within our own minds. There are also battles raging over control of our attention spans, our emotions, our behavioural and our biometric data. Access to big, bigger, biggest data (or lack thereof) can determine the success or failure of organizations and nations. In this essay, we explore the increasingly high-stakes financial – and physical – threats the modern age of cyberwarfare poses to businesses, to individuals and to society.

You will be a casualty of a war you may not even be aware of: *Cybersecurity, war and the role of civilians.*

I'm afraid it's too late: you have already been drafted into a global war and you will be, or already have been, a casualty. The war around you is the one being fought online, in the news media and, potentially, in space. In this war, global powers are stealing your information and your attention and impacting how you live your life. The impact can be shrugged off by thinking that privacy is dead, that you make your own opinions and that those big power politics don't impact your day-to-day life. You are wrong.

Recent research from the Center for Strategic and International Studies examined cyberespionage and cyberwar data on China, North Korea, Iran, India, Russia, the United Kingdom, the United States, Germany, Australia, Japan, South Korea, Ukraine, Israel and France, with the rest of the world listed as a separate category.[34] The study named the rest of the world as the third-worst offender, with 67 incidents. Next in the ranking came Iran with 44 incidents, and North Korea with 38. India was listed as guilty of 16 important cyber incidents from 2006 to 2018, while the US was accused of nine. However, Russia has been responsible for 98 major cyber incidents since 2006, with losses of more than $1 million each. And from 2006 to 2018, China was involved in 108 cyber incidents with losses of more than $1 million each, including conducting cyberespionage spying on 12 countries and stealing information from hundreds of millions of customers of a US hotel chain.

These nation-state attacks can involve, but are not limited to, stealing citizens' private information and selling it online, propaganda wars intended to destabilize entire national systems,[35] corporate espionage intended to ensure

[34]CSIS, 2020 'Significant Cyber Incidents'. Available from: www.csis.org/programs/cybersecurity-and-governance/technology-policy-program/other-projects-cybersecurity

[35]P.W. Singer and Emerson T. Brooking, *LikeWar: The Weaponization of Social Media* (New York: Mariner Books, 2018)

national-level economic success[36] and tracking and censorship activities that enable intelligence units to better operate in other theatres. In these wars, offensive and defensive attacks happen in both minutes and over years, and occasionally they spill from the cyber domain into the real world. Cyberwar can beget kinetic war, but this is rare – more often, it accompanies other tactics.[37]

Cyberwar has become normalized as a war-fighting tactic and we are seeing an increase in military units focused on cyberwar.[38] It costs less, for one thing. It's less obvious to citizens, for another. It has complicated rules of engagement and a lack of legal precedent,[39] which makes it acceptable for nations to engage in without too much threat of retribution or attack. And in part, because it's so hard to verify who is actually behind an attack, it is very hard to effectively punish any attacker.[40] Plus, the victims are often individuals and corporations who pay in information stolen rather than physical casualties. There is simply nothing to see. The lack of visual evidence combined with low or

[36]Sherisse Pham, 'How Much Has the US Lost from China's IP Theft?', CNN, 23 March 2018. Available from: money.cnn.com/2018/03/23/technology/china-us-trump-tariffs-ip-theft/index.html

[37]Erica D. Borghard and Shawn W. Lonergan, 'The Logic of Cohersion in Cyberspace', Security Studies 26:3, 2017. Available from: www.tandfonline.com/doi/abs/10.1080/0 9636412.2017.1306396?scroll=top&needAccess=true&journalCode=fsst20

[38]Keith Breene, 'Who are the cyberwar superpowers?', World Economic Forum, 4 May 2016. Available from: www.weforum.org/agenda/2016/05/who-are-the-cyber-war-superpowers/

[39]Tarah Wheeler, 'In Cyberwar, There Are No Rules', Foreign Policy, 12 September 2018. Available from: foreignpolicy.com/2018/09/12/in-cyberwar-there-are-no-rules-cybersecurity-war-defense/

[40]Lily Hay Newman, 'Hacker Lexicon: What is the Attribution Problem?', Wired, 24 December 2016. Available from:. www.wired.com/2016/12/hacker-lexicon-attribu-tion-problem/

unattributable mortality rates means that there has been little collective awareness, action or intermediation against this type of conflict.

We (average citizens) are all walking around unaware, while around us our governments are playing war.

Citizens, globally, may be able to ignore cyberwars now. But these wars will metastasize and change in both the nature of the target and its capabilities. Deepfake video technology will pervade our media.[41] We will no longer be able to trust the old adage of seeing is believing. Cybercrimes will inflict more damage,[42] particularly as we see an increase on targets like electrical grids. When we lose power and critical infrastructure, the insidious nature of our shadow war will start to take real human lives. And when we start to fight cyberwars in space,[43] we will need to worry about how easy it is to destroy the very foundations of our society.

And I'm afraid it is too late: war in space is inevitable.[44] The US Department of Defense is spending tens of billions of dollars on their Space Force.[45] And so too are many other

[41]Simon Parkin, 'Politicians Fear This Like Fire', *Guardian*, 22 June 2019. Available from: www.theguardian.com/technology/ng-interactive/2019/jun/22/the-rise-of-the-deepfake-and-the-threat-to-democracy

[42]Marc Wilczek, 'Cybercrime is increasing and more costly for organizations', CIO, 2 April 2019. Available from: www.cio.com/article/3386417/cybercrime-is-increasing-and-more-costly-for-organizations.html

[43]Danny Palmer, 'Cyberwarfare in space: Satellites at risk of hacker attacks', ZDNet, 2 July 2019. Available from: www.zdnet.com/article/cyberwarfare-in-space-satellites-at-risk-of-hacker-attacks/

[44]Dr Beyza Unal, 'Cybersecurity of NATO's Space-based Strategic Assets', Chatham House, 1 July 2019. Available from:. www.chathamhouse.org/publication/cybersecurity-nato-s-space-based-strategic-assets#

[45]Otso Rajala, 'High Ambitions: Superpowers and the Weaponization of Outer Space', The Perspective, 14 April 2016. Available from: www.theperspective.se/high-ambitions-superpowers-and-the-weaponization-of-outer-space

countries. All of whom understand that our global satellite infrastructure is extremely fragile and vulnerable. Russia has already used satellite infrastructure during conflicts in Syria and Ukraine to jam GPS signals of remotely piloted aircraft in order to ground them. And both China and Russia can conduct cyberattacks with little risk to their own satellite and infrastructure systems. Additionally, governments have very little ability to look at the situational surroundings of space and to track and monitor space-based activities.[46] Furthermore, global legal frameworks for space are antiquated and abhorrently unprepared to deal with an issue of war in space and superpower nations are unwilling to update or sign new space-based treaties that limit their actions in space – many with defensible reasoning: economic, political and security in nature (2018).[47] Nations want as much leniency as possible to do whatever they want to ensure that they have the advantage in this new domain.

When war in space comes, it will have the potential to have massive impacts on Earth. In an extreme but not unfathomable scenario, a single satellite could, intentionally or otherwise, crash into other satellites and create a destructive garbage patch of debris around the planet. This concern, known as the Kessler syndrome,[48] has been discussed since 1978. The reality is more and more likely now, as thousands

---

[46]Major Erin Salinas, 'Space Situational Awareness is Space Battle Management', Air Force Space Command, 16 May 2018. Available from: www.afspc.af.mil/News/Article-Display/Article/1523196/space-situational-awareness-is-space-battle-management/

[47]Editorial Board, 'The world should update its laws on outer space', *Financial Times*, 2018. Available from: www.ft.com/content/d67ffecc-02dc-11e9-9d01-cd4d49afbbe3

[48]Louis de Gouyon Matignon, 'The Kessler Syndrome', Space Legal Issues, 27 March 2019. Available from: www.spacelegalissues.com/space-law-the-kessler-syndrome/

more satellites enter lower earth orbit.[49] The fear is that this destructive garbage patch could take out all satellite communications and potentially the satellites themselves, which would mean that we no longer have weather data, emergency management data, payment systems, and a slew of other communications networks that we deem essential to life on Earth. When we lose those systems, we will effectively have to rethink how we live, transport ourselves, communicate, pay for services, and more. And the big end result is that citizens will be casualties of a war that they might not even have been informed was happening.

While global governments are playing secret war games in cyberspace, citizens need to – and can – rethink how much leniency they want to give to governments and how much transparency there should be about global conflicts. Now is the moment to decide how governments should operate and how we should define conflict, who should know about conflict and what tactics are acceptable as a means to protect territories, economies and, ultimately, our species. I believe that the only resilient system is one in which all people are aware of and understand the basic rules for the conflicts that are impacting the world.

As people look forward to space policy, cybersecurity policy and general systems for global living, it is important to re-evaluate the systems that underlie how our governments work but also the united collective spirit of our existence. To do that, there is a need for a collective moment of deep moral realignment. In short, we need to think about what

[49]Michael Sheetz and Magdalena Petrova, 'Why in the next decade companies will launch thousands more satellites than in all of history', CNBC, 15 December 2019. Available from:.www.cnbc.com/2019/12/14/spacex-oneweb-and-amazon-to-launch-thousands-more-satellites-in-2020s.html

the values are that underlie our global society. When we identify those values, we need to build systems that better reflect them.

Cyberwarfare isn't a nation-state issue, it's a human issue.

If we believe it's OK to lose privacy to ensure an increase in national power, if we believe it's OK to risk our current technology-dependent infrastructure systems to gather more political dominance in space, if we believe that human lives are less important than the health of a nation, then our current policies are just fine. I am not sure that that is what people really do believe.

If the victims of conflict are society writ large, then we need to assess what that says about how we think about ourselves. Citizens need to decide if a government that acts in its own best interest, and not in the interest of its people, is the type of government that is needed. When hundreds of billions of dollars' worth of intellectual property[50] and personal information is lost each year and the recourse is found in insurance claims and not governance, it is time to ask if this is the world that best suits its constituents.

If citizens have the opportunity to participate in government, they need to take it. We must fight to ensure that our society is deeply reflective of our values, our morals and our desires. If we do not want to end up conscripted into and casualties of a war we do not understand, we need to demand that the government explains its international positioning and the methods for its action. Like nuclear weapons strategies

[50]Sherisse Pham, 'How much has the US lost from China's IP theft?', CNN, 23 March 2018. Available from: money.cnn.com/2018/03/23/technology/china-us-trump-tariffs-ip-theft/index.html

and disarmament policy,[51] we can lessen the acceptability of cyberwar as a strategy of national policy.

To reduce reliance on and acceptability of cyberwar, there must be a coalescence of public opinion around the acceptability of the tactic and an understanding for when and how we deem it an appropriate engagement strategy. To generate public opinion, there needs to be more regular convening in our communities and nationally about the idea of cyberwar and an understanding of what it involves, how it is fought and potential casualties.

It is unacceptable for governments to risk our lives because they have not been asked to limit their power. However, the only people who can limit governments are citizens. Therefore, citizens must understand the dangers and lobby for those dangers to be mediated and for governments globally to be more careful in the risks that these weapons pose to our lives.

[51]Nuclear Threat Initiative, 'Nuclear Disarmament Resource Collection', Nuclear Threat Initiative, 7 August 2018. Available from: www.nti.org/analysis/reports/nuclear-disarmament/

7

A Foreshadow of the Future Economy

By David Tal, founder and Senior Strategic Foresight Consultant at Quantumrun Foresight

This chapter explores the ramifications of accelerated automation, and the parallel emergence of radical new economic models based on ideas that have been 'lying around', waiting for their chance to change the world. In particular, the chapter looks at the impact universal basic incomes could have on the industries and economies of the future, and why interventions today could dramatically change the world for a better tomorrow.

The year 2020 will be remembered as an eye-opening tipping point and maybe even an early glimpse into our collective futures. On the whole, the world's nations entered that year with troublesome levels of corporate-held debt,[52] historic

---

[52]'Rising corporate debt: Should we worry?', *Deloitte*, 15 April 2019. Available from: www2.deloitte.com/us/en/insights/economy/issues-by-the-numbers/rising-corporate-debt-levels.html

wealth inequality,[53] rising un- and underemployment (in part) due to globalization and automation,[54] worsening climate change,[55] paralyzing political polarization, surging growth in anti-democratic populist leaders,[56] rapid cultural change... and then came the COVID-19 pandemic.[57]

The unique nature of this virus, especially its ability to lay dormant but stay infectious for weeks before causing health complications in its victims, led to its frightening and compounding growth rate. However, what was truly stunning and poignant about this pandemic was how it very rapidly laid bare the fragility of our governments, our businesses, our economies and, ultimately, our individual beliefs and way of life.

COVID-19 was a threat that China's entire propaganda regime was powerless to conceal; that the United States' expensive military superiority could not target a bullet at; that Europe's bureaucrats and technocrats could not negotiate with. Meanwhile, this pandemic reminded each of us of our mortality, the importance of our social ties, and our

[53]Christopher Ingraham, 'Massive new data set suggests inequality is about to get even worse', *Washington Post*, 4 January 2018. Available from: www.washington-post.com/news/wonk/wp/2018/01/04/massive-new-data-set-suggests-inequality-is-about-to-get-even-worse/

[54]Mark Muro et al., 'Automation perpetuates the red-blue divide', Brookings, 19 March 2019. Available from: www.brookings.edu/blog/the-avenue/2019/03/25/automation-perpetuates-the-red-blue-divide/

[55]Chelsea Harvey, 'C02 Levels Just Hit Another Record—Here's Why it Matters', *Scientific American*, 16 May 2019. Available from: www.scientificamerican.com/article/co2-levels-just-hit-another-record-heres-why-it-matters/

[56]Frederick Kempe, 'Democracies are on track to lose their global economic dominance as "authoritarian capitalism" rises', CNBC, 6 July 2019. Available from: www.cnbc.com/2019/07/05/democracies-are-on-track-to-lose-their-global-economic-dominance.html

[57]World Health Organization, 2019. Novel Coronavirus, 2019. Available from: www.who.int/emergencies/diseases/novel-coronavirus-2019

dependence on a large breadth of societal systems outside of our control.

In brief, by mid-February 2020, fear of the pandemic caused world stock markets to crash; weeks later, tens of millions of workers were laid off or furloughed; governments (depending on the country) adopted increasingly authoritarian measures to enforce social distancing practices on the general populace, all while national health systems were stretched to their breaking points. Throughout this process, a large number of inconvenient truths became glaringly obvious:

- Universal access to affordable healthcare must be a human right;
- Dependence on employer-provided benefits is an unreliable social safety net;
- Funding and support for essential services had been sorely lacking;
- Workers once viewed as disposable or replaceable were suddenly classified as essential;
- A substantial percentage of small- and medium-sized businesses could not survive a month without income;
- Even worse, an unsettling majority of our respective populations could not survive a month without income.

And it was this last point that ended up being the most concerning realization for most people. The reality is that if the vast majority of the population could afford to simply stay home for a month or more, then the spread of the virus could have been significantly minimized and contained much faster than it was. This statement is an oversimplification to be sure, but it is unfair to expect the majority of the population to make rational decisions about their society's collective health if that same majority feels their individual financial security is at risk.

Governments at all levels recognized this reality, which is why so many began to consider various options to support individuals with financial aid. The historic, $2 trillion, Coronavirus Aid, Relief, and Economic Security (CARES) Act, approved by the United States government, sent individuals earning less than $75,000 an emergency cash grant of $1,200.[58] The Canada Emergency Response Benefit (CERB), approved by the Canadian government, sent $2,000 for four months to workers who lost their incomes due to COVID-related business shutdowns.[59] Other nations like South Korea[60] and India[61] also approved emergency funds to send individuals cash payments, as well as care packages in the form of food staples.

All of these examples and more involved direct cash transfers to individuals, a government action not too dissimilar from the contentious idea of the Universal Basic Income (UBI).

[58]Kelsey Snell, 'What's Inside the Senate's $2 Trillion Coronavirus Aid Package', NPR, 26 March 2020. Available from: www.npr.org/2020/03/26/821457551/whats-inside-the-senate-s-2-trillion-coronavirus-aid-package

[59]John Paul Tasker, 'Parliament passes Ottawa's $107 billion COVID-19 aid package', CBC News, 2020. Available from: www.cbc.ca/news/politics/covid19-coronavirus-ottawa-hill-economic-legislation-1.5509178

[60]Sangmi Cha and Hyonhee Shin, 'South Korea to pay families hundreds of dollars to ease coronavirus impact', The Star, 30 March 2020. Available from: www.thestar.com.my/news/world/2020/03/30/south-korea-coronavirus-cases-rise-steadily-more-financial-aid-expected

[61]Saheli Roy Choudhury, 'India announces $22.5 billion stimulus package to help those affected by the lockdown', CNBC, 26 March 2020. Available from: www.cnbc.com/2020/03/26/coronavirus-india-needs-a-support-package-larger-than-20-billion-dollars.html

Very simply, a UBI is an income granted to all citizens (rich and poor) individually and unconditionally, i.e. without a means test or work requirement. It's the government giving you free money every month.

In 1967, Martin Luther King Jr. said, 'The solution to poverty is to abolish it directly by a now widely discussed measure: the guaranteed income.'[62] And he's not the only one who has made this argument. Nobel Prize economists, including Milton Friedman[63] and F.A. Hayek,[64] among others, have also supported various forms of the UBI. US president Richard Nixon[65] even tried to pass a version of the UBI in 1969, albeit unsuccessfully.

Over the past several decades, the UBI has remained a popular policy idea among select progressives and conservatives, but has often been described as too radical an idea to be taken seriously. The policy has further suffered from vague and unsubstantiated claims that giving people free money would damage their self-worth or disincentivize

[62]Jordan Weissman, 'Martin Luther King's Economic Dream: A Guaranteed Income for All Americans', *The Atlantic*, 28 August 2013. Available from: www.theatlantic.com/business/archive/2013/08/martin-luther-kings-economic-dream-a-guaranteed-income-for-all-americans/279147/

[63]Sam Bowman, 'Milton Friedman on the Negative Income Tax', Adam Smith Institute, 31 July 2013. Available from: www.adamsmith.org/blog/welfare-pensions/milton-friedman-on-the-negative-income-tax

[64]Matt Zwolinski, 'A Hayekian Case for Free Markets and a Basic Income', University of San Diego, 14 June 2019. Available from: papers.ssrn.com/sol3/papers.cfm?abstract_id=3396791

[65]Mike Alberti and Kevin C. Brown, 'Guaranteed income's moment in the sun', Remapping Debate, 24 April 2013. Available from: www.remappingdebate.org/sites/default/files/Guaranteed per cent20income's per cent20moment per cent20in per cent20the per cent20sun_0.pdf

people from working – claims that numerous studies have repeatedly refuted.[66,67,68]

And yet, despite its stigma, in 2020, governments handing out money to its citizens suddenly became politically and economically practical, and very much urgent. And the reasons why this perspective shift occurred will stand as a sobering case study that may very well foreshadow our collective futures.

FORESHADOWING OUR FUTURE ECONOMY

Let's consider that what this pandemic did, in very short order, was to force millions out of work and leave a relatively few 'essential workers' employed to keep basic society functioning. Most businesses that involved physical human interaction were forced to shut down, and even those companies that could operate remotely saw massive revenue losses. In other words, it became very apparent that the economy did not function solely on the online purchases of the wealthy few, but instead by the economic activity of the broad majority of the population.

---

[66]Damon Jones and Ioana Elena Marinescu, 'The Labor Market Impacts of Universal and Permanent Cash Transfers: Evidence from the Alaska Permanent Fund', University of Chicago/University of Pennsylvania, 22 February 2018. Available from: papers.ssrn.com/sol3/papers.cfm?abstract_id=3118343

[67]Joshua Howgego, 'Universal income study finds money for nothing won't make us work less', *New Scientist*, 8 February 2019. Available from: www.newscientist.com/article/2193136-universal-income-study-finds-money-for-nothing-wont-make-us-work-less/

[68]Christopher Blattman et al., 'Generating Skilled Self-Employment in Developing Countries: Experimental Evidence from Uganda', *Quarterly Journal of Economics*, 23 May 2013. Available from: papers.ssrn.com/sol3/papers.cfm?abstract_id=2268552

Now, as a thought experiment, let's replace the pandemic with the steady and compounding progression and application of automation software and robotics in our collective workplaces. Would it be unreasonable to foresee a day over the coming decades where technology progresses to a point where it automates the work of most people's jobs, resulting in the employment of only a minority of highly trained, versatile, 'essential workers'? And should this future scenario become a reality, would it then be unreasonable to believe that (like in 2020), an economy designed around mass consumption would **not** sustain itself under the buying power of a shrinking labour market, let alone a labour market composed entirely of essential workers?

In this scenario, it would then be reasonable to expect that to avoid a future, technology-driven economic recession, future politicians would need to either devise a radically new and inverted economic system that thrives on a shrinking base of consumers or they would (again, like in 2020) inject artificial spending power directly into the general population. As you might imagine, such future politicians would likely choose the latter option, both for political expediency and also to avoid a popular revolt.

In other words, a new era of big governments is on the horizon.

THE POST-PANDEMIC DECADE

While the thinking during the pandemic scare was that the world would *never* be the same, the reality is that the post-COVID-19 world will likely be *more* of the same, just accelerated.

For example, during and after every economic recession, companies take stock of their operations and seize opportunities to cut costs and introduce efficiencies. This means that the 2020s will likely see more (not fewer) early retirement buyouts, investments in robotics for physical labour automation, investments in artificial-intelligence-driven software solutions for the automation of cognitive tasks, use of on-demand freelance labour (virtual and physical), and the increased use of remote work solutions. Again, nothing new here, but as these trends accelerate, 'traditional', well-paying employment will likely become more tenuous and less abundant.

This increased investment into automation also has the potential to eventually negate the need for low-cost, foreign human labour, thereby limiting or reversing the advantage of outsourcing operations internationally. And remarkably, the COVID-19 event may even accelerate this trend as well.

For example, the pandemic highlighted how the over-concentration of manufacturing in developing nations impaired the ability of developed nations to effectively protect their citizens' health. This realization may potentially see a partial reversal of globalization trends during the 2020s that will see the manufacturing of vital goods (like pharmaceuticals and medical supplies, *to start*) be insourced back within developed countries. Unfortunately, even if this insourcing trend becomes a reality, the automation trends discussed earlier still apply, meaning that any insourced manufacturing will likely result in marginal employment growth long term.

So, what are the solutions left to society?

Are we doomed to end up living lives as un- or underemployed consumers spending government-provided

UBI stipends? Will society instead generate an enormous bounty of new job options accessible to the masses, regardless of age or educational attainment? Or (my personal hope) will it be possible for nations to use automation to reach a level of economic abundance where providing for basic human needs becomes inconsequentially cheap and professional pursuits become a choice rather than an obligation for all?

8

The African Opportunity

By Dali Tembo, Afrofuturist and Co-Founder of The Culture Foundry

By 2050, one in four humans on Earth will be African. This means the history of humanity has come full circle. The future, just like the cradle, of humankind is centred on the African continent. Africa is youthful and hopeful, unlike the ageing postalgia-plagued, self-flagellating WEIRD (Western, Educated, Industrialized, Rich, Developed) world. However, Africa is misunderstood by the wider world and held back by institutional weakness and persistent political problems. In this essay, Dali unpacks how the world has got wrong about 'Africa' (for one thing, it's a vibrant continent made up of diverse nations, and rich, colourful subcultures, not a homogeneous place) and explores the opportunities ahead for an African cultural and economic renaissance, the likes of which the world has never seen before.

Dear future generations,

What I'm about to tell you will almost certainly sound like something you've heard before. But hear me out! There's something to be said for exploring the same subject over and over again, particularly if it averts repeating aspects of our history defined by the absence of critical thinking. If we don't learn from the mistakes we've made in the past, we are bound to slip when passing on the proverbial intergenerational knowledge baton. Young Africans will inherit one of the largest continents on Earth: one that is bigger than China, Japan, India, America and the whole of Europe put together. And yet they will also be bequeathed with generations' worth of stigmas, myths and misconceptions, most notably about the continent's ability to develop beyond what the West sees as 'typical' of the Third World.

The sheer number of ill-informed decision makers applying their trade from Western-based businesses, with influence on the continent, is astounding. Despite the emergence of African voices in business, politics and popular culture, the positioning of Africa's global narrative overseas still often depends on folks whose levels of discernment about the continent remain questionable – insert conversations confusing Niger with Nigeria, for example. The outdated way in which African countries are portrayed, and the opportunities within them maligned, is not particularly surprising.

Most research I've encountered on the continent's opportunities has depended (almost exclusively) on quantitative data. Although valuable in isolation, quants lacks the empathy required to unlock the whys behind the whats. This context really does matter, particularly when we know that bad news sells. Nuance is all too often lost or misinterpreted when information is taken out of its original context. The challenge, therefore, for those of us attempting to light a torch on more balanced perspectives on Africa is to sidestep labels that have been used to discredit – like 'Afro-optimist', for example. My objective is not simply to share the optimistic perspective on Africa, but rather to acknowledge our difficulties and opportunities in the same light.

One way of retaining some credibility may be to face some of the challenges Africa still faces prior to painting any portrait of the continent. Despite significant developments over the last 20 years, for example, we're still struggling to offer basic services like clean water, education and food security to the one in three people living on or below the poverty line. Increases in political stability in some countries have not eradicated war (as observed with conflicts in Burkina Faso and Nigeria, as recently as 2019). We also still see evidence of corruption, particularly around election time, in many countries, made even more complex by our over-reliance on single commodity economic structures – something we saw the effects of in 2007 and again more recently during the coronavirus pandemic. These are all real problems and no one is denying them – particularly in the face of constant reinforcement from media houses.

AFRICAN RESILIENCE

First, one of the hallmarks of the young African's perspective is irrefutable optimism in the face of seemingly insurmountable odds. I'll always remember partnering with the UCT Unilever Institute of Strategic Marketing in 2018, and presenting one of the biggest Youth Reports ever released on the state of South African Youth. It was devastating to hear young voices (15 to 24 years old) express the burdens of unemployment (more than 55 per cent at the time) and exposing significant gaps in education (only 33 per cent of school entrants eventually become tertiary eligible).

Despite this, I have found when investigating African markets, and asking how young people feel about their futures, the overwhelming majority replied optimistically – expecting their standard of living to improve. These youths no longer look up to governments (or formalized traditional institutions) with the same devotion or hope that was exhibited by previous generations. To them, their futures are firmly in their own hands and will be the product of self-navigation, internet access, 'the hustle' and entrepreneurship. While one should never romanticize survival tactics, it's hard not to acknowledge that this level of resistance to pessimism is unique to Africans, and a critically important differentiator for any business looking for a robust and loyal future customer.

AFRICAN INNOVATION

Second, one of the biggest misconceptions about African consumers is premised on the idea that they are happy to consume standardized, cheap and below par brands and products. What this 'good enough' mentality fails to understand is the death of the traditional trend adoption curve. While trends and innovation may have run from the 'haves' to the 'have-nots' in the past, today the most influential ideas in culture stem from Africa's middle- to low-income earners and the informal settlements; think M-Pesa from Kenya, reportedly created by Kenyan student Nyagaka Anyona Ouko, and Vodacom's Please Call Me service – designed by a 24-year-old South African, Nkosana Makate.

The examples above show that Africans don't want to blindly accept what's worked in other markets, and are demanding local solutions for local problems. This should also explain why international governments, businesses and non-profits are investing in African people today, more than ever before. The 'chaos' and randomness of everyday life on the continent is not a barrier towards innovation; increasingly, it's proving to be the catalyst. Don't believe me? Visit Yabacon, Lagos's version of Silicon Valley. If that doesn't work, you're more than welcome to seek out some of the 642 tech hubs flourishing across the continent.

The arts also present one of the most illustrative ways of seeing this African innovation at work. In recent years, the *Billboard* Hot 100 list has consistently presented us with new and pioneering sounds stemming from all over Africa. Just take the major successes of now famous artists like Black Coffee (from South Africa) and Burna Boy (from Nigeria) as examples. To quote Jay-Z, this is not something we're only seeing in the music business; Africans are also involved in the 'business' of making music. We have witnessed the rise of proudly African streaming services like Boomplay and seen increased interest in major labels like Roc-A-Fella, Universal and Sony in finding and supporting innovative new local artists and sounds.

AFRICA'S POPULATION GROWTH

Here's a question that's gaining a lot of popularity at the moment: what would you guess is the number of multinational companies on the continent today earning an annual revenue of 1 billion dollars or more? Well, given the challenges discussed earlier, you would be forgiven for erring on the side of caution with a response like 'under 100?' In reality, there are more than 400 companies grossing over 1 billion dollars and they all share one particularly interesting characteristic – they see the youth bulge and population growth in Africa as an opportunity, not a hindrance.

Africa has one of the highest population growth rates, at 2.7 per cent a year. Its corresponding urbanization growth rates are not far behind, accounting for over 80 per cent of the estimated $6.7 trillion in current consumer spending. These figures really start to make an impact when you consider that a third of the world's global youth will live in sub-Saharan Africa by 2050.[69] If my generation thought their CVs needed to stand out, you can imagine what future generations will have to do to make an impression among this level of competition. More importantly, most developed countries are seeing significant reductions in the size of their potential markets, at exactly the same time. China's population, for example, is projected to decrease by 31.4 million by 2050.[70] If you're future-focused, and looking for people who see their ability to be competitive as a necessity for survival, where would you be putting your money?

Of course, challenges exist when it comes to servicing this new urban population; however, these obstacles come with vast opportunities for those willing to think outside the box. Essentially, population growth and urbanization could mean improving regional integration, making market access easier and expanding the workforce to power Africa's growth.

[69]Brookings, 2019. Foresight Africa: Top Priorities for the Continent in 2019, Bookings, Available from: https://www.brookings.edu/multi-chapter-report/foresight-africa-top-priorities-for-the-continent-in-2019/

[70]UN, 17 June 2019. 'Growing at a slower pace, world population is expected to reach 9.7 billion in 2050 and could peak at nearly 11 billion around 2100', UN, Available from:https://www.un.org/development/desa/en/news/population/world-population-prospects-2019.html

AFRICA'S SECRET WEAPON

One of the most exciting developments I've observed in recent years has been a shift in the conversation about the importance of women in contributing to Africa's future success. Gender equality is not just a social or 'labour market' issue. It takes a rare and uniquely uninformed mind to believe that 50 per cent of the continent's potential working population contributing to the economy might be a bad idea. It's no secret that Africa's women have been curtailed significantly by the presence of social, political, economic and cultural constraints, most notably in the lowest of low-income countries and as a result of colonialism's emphasis on cash crops, perceptions around religion, and gender discrimination in the workplace.

Increasingly, however, due to increased access to education and innovations in the realm of medicine, women are breaking these stereotypes. According to the World Bank, roughly two-thirds of all African women are now working in either the formal or informal sectors. Those of us who travel and see the impact of this on society at large would argue these numbers may actually be even larger, particularly when you see the breakdown of traditional male roles in conservative societies. Here, women often make up more than half of all entrepreneurs, and are taking up spaces as senior business leaders, religious figures, politicians and even high-ranking military.

This generation has seen an abundance of African firsts: the first female presidents, the first Nobel Peace Prize winner, the first Forbes' wealthiest woman, and a host of other globally renowned leading female first scientists, artists and entrepreneurs. Emerging role models like these women will continue to inspire African women of the future. Their contributions are not just significant, they provide a vision of the future that one gender couldn't possibly carry and also help us to understand why the World Economic Forum's 2019 Global Competitiveness Index cites places like Kenya, Rwanda, Morocco, Mauritius, South Africa, Botswana, Namibia, Tunisia, Algeria, Egypt and the Seychelles, all in the top hundred. Long may the influence of African females continue to grow.

In conclusion, Michael Joseph, founding CEO of Safaricom, once said: 'If we applied Western standards to all the things we do, we would probably still be in the dark ages.' It should come as no surprise then that the recently released list of the fastest-growing economies in 2020 has no country from Europe or America and six from Africa. Now is the time. If there is one thing to take away from my experience, it is that we are getting rid of our inferiority complex. Future ambassadors – that's you – have a critical role to play going forward in assisting to paint a more holistic perspective of the continent to potential investors. Our continent should not rely on osmosis for perceptions to change when so many of you have the capacity to be influential. Essentially, change is always possible if people feel they are involved. My appeal attempts to do just that – encourage involvement. The rest of the world will only see Africa differently when we take control of the narrative and help to explain how we're advancing political, social and economic gains achieved over the last few decades, despite the challenges.

9

No Money Beyond Mars

By Mathana, technology ethicist and futurist

Space settlements are slowly but surely becoming a viable possibility for the future of the human race. However, before we go and set up our extraterrestrial home in the stars, we need to make sure we are not carrying our old problems with us. We need to explore new economic models; as humanity evolves beyond Earth, there is no reason to carry our old, outdated, inequitable economic systems with us. We need to explore radical futures beyond money and ownership as we know it today.

Imagination is a gift from the cosmos. I don't know *how*, but I have a suspicion that human DNA is somehow encoded with an impetus to ask 'why?' Whether a trait of sentient consciousness or an evolutionary fluke, humanity's inquisitiveness represents not only a fascinating anomaly of carbon-based life forms but also a feature that seems to be unique in the cosmos. As the American astronomer Carl Sagan said, 'we are the universe observing itself', and as our points of observation keep expanding, the orders of our perceived awareness cascade in unprecedented ways. Our origin is humble, but our journey profound: from cave dwelling to subsistence agriculture to industrialization to digitalization – a time in which our species is now capable of leaving our home world. From those early caves, recognizing the importance of the question 'why?' has been key to our understanding of the profound: the meaning of invention, the calling of discovery, the joy of creation and the dignity of exploration.

To look to humanity's future, it is prudent to look to our past. Stories about the night sky have been a constant feature of every culture throughout history. These are examples of humanity's enduring curiosity about the origin of life and the nature of the universe, which has instilled in us a constant desire to explore, discover and traverse new environments. Star charts for seacraft navigation have given way to spacecraft navigation in a sea of stars, yet the urge to discover persists through generations.

Trajectories of exploration are sometimes exponential. In 1610, Galileo Galilei pointed a newly patented technology to the heavens and saw a celestial body as it had never been seen before. Galilei's telescopic observation of Mars was the closest detailed inspection that any human eyes had ever given the Martian surface. Just over 350 years later, in 1965, NASA's *Mariner 4* made the first approach to Mars, and then in 1976, *Viking 1* completed the first successful soft landing on the Martian surface. From our first inspection of Mars, it took humanity less than 400 years to both land something on its surface and create a human presence in space. Since 2000, humans have sustained a continually inhabited off-Earth presence aboard the International Space Station. Not content with visiting our own solar system, we explore on: in 2016,

NASA's Dawn mission provided an intimate view of a new world when it danced around the orbit of ice-rich Ceres, a recently classified 'dwarf planet' that lies in the asteroid belt between Mars and Jupiter.

The famous 'Golden Records' affixed to the two *Voyager* spacecraft launched in 1977 were a deliberate attempt by Sagan and others to preserve and share messages in interstellar bottles. Forty years later, both *Voyager* spacecraft, those first shouts into the cosmic cave, continue unabated on their journeys, where they may sail through the vacuum of deep space for aeons. Of the five spacecraft that have left the solar system, or are on a trajectory to do so, four (*Pioneers 10 and 11, Voyagers 1 and 2*) carry what NASA calls a 'message from humanity to the cosmos'. While contact with the Pioneers has now been lost, their presence still matters. They serve as a sort of celestial remnant of our species. While they may no longer be intermediaries of discovery, they are still vectors of exploration; tiny objects floating through the vast vacuum of space, carrying sights and sounds of humanity like a message in a bottle.

Our journeys of discovery continue to break boundaries of what we thought were established systems. From the Bohr model of an atom, to the planetary orbits of our solar system, to the observable universe, all around and through us is rotation and expansion, yet the forces that hold our universe together are still being explored. Our solar system is part of a vast cosmic dance, spinning around the galactic centre, completing a rotation approximately every 230 million years.

Calculations of universal cartography still leave mysteries to be unravelled, hidden forces to be revealed and gravity theory to be ironed out, but when we talk about our own solar system, astro-geometry becomes a bit more comprehensible.

Astronomers measure distances in our solar system (and beyond) in 'astronomical units', or what is known as an 'AU', which we have set as the average distance of Earth from the Sun, or just under 150,000,000km.

Some 100 kilometres over our heads, a different boundary region exists: a divide between the edge of Earth's atmosphere and outer space (sometimes called the Kármán Line). It is both a practical and a scientific border. With a Z-axis demarcation comes a new type of regulatory regime and jurisdiction – below it fly aircraft, above it, spacecraft.

Building for the new domain of spacecraft requires a new set of research ethics. While our technological advancements have exponentially developed to the rocket age, our bodies remain biologically and cognitively formed and conditioned for (and by) life on our homeworld.

Several experiments have been carried out to assess the psychological, sociological and physiological impact of prolonged isolation; however, such simulations can only attempt to replicate conditions that would be faced by humans on extended journeys. Prolonged habitation in space could have a profound impact on both our physical and mental health. This includes exposure to radiation, dysregulations in immunity, an increased risk of both cancer and latent viral reactivation. Physiological effects include changes to brain volume, deformation of the pituitary 'master' gland, and ocular complications.

While many physiological anomalies have been observed in those who have spent substantial time on the ISS, humans lack a clear understanding of the long-term health risks of low gravity and solar radiation. We also don't have a grasp on the impact that space habitation would have on human reproduction and developmental psychology conditions.

The ethical hurdles to studying the effects of zero gravity on pregnancy and neonatal development remain significant.

For all we know about atoms and biology and pulsars, there are so many more unknowns. Our understanding of the long-term effects of space on the human mind and body is still very limited. While humans have had a continual presence on the International Space Station since 2000, the longest continuous time that a human has spent in space is 438 days (Valery Polyakov, aboard Mir),[71] and the most time in total spent by any human is still less than three years (Gennady Padalka spent 878 days in space over five flights[72]). Four hundred days pales in comparison to the 40 years it took *Voyagers 1* and *2* to reach interstellar space. While such a timeframe may be a cosmic blip, a crewed space journey into interstellar space would require spending a substantial portion of one's lifespan on a confined spacecraft with limited resources.

Early astronauts are still alive today; within living memory we have turned a ceiling into a semi-permeable membrane. But that window to space is fragile, so constant safety monitoring and sustainable decommissioning should be considered part of the life cycle of all Earth-orbiting satellites. An unprecarious ascent through Earth's gravitational grasp and a boundary to the notions of country and company is necessary for futurist ideas to prosper.

Existential threats range from nuclear weapons to climate change and even killer robots. Humanity requires a robust

[71] Britannica, Valery Vladimirovich Polyakov. Available from: www.britannica.com/biography/Valery-Vladimirovich-Polyakov

[72] Alec Luhn, 'Russian cosmonaut beats record for career time spent in space', *Guardian*, 29 June 2015. Available from: www.theguardian.com/science/2015/jun/29/russian-cosmonaut-record-time-in-space-gennady-padalka

redundancy, and until humanity establishes off-world habitation, Earth remains a single point of failure for our species. Robert Oppenheimer shepherded the experimentation that led to the exploitation of the atom. With the advent of the nuclear bomb, humanity figured out the very big implications of a controlled break of a small atom. We should not forget how profound it is that our species has the ability to end all life as we know it. So perhaps Oppenheimer was prescient to paraphrase the god Vishnu in his utterances in the Bhagavad Gita after witnessing the first ever detonation of a nuclear bomb: 'Now I am becoming Death, the destroyer of worlds'.

Our species takes its finger off the button of a device that we only recently created, but one that has the destructive capacity of no other before it. It's within our grasp to leave not a legacy, but rather a passive indication that the order found by future generations was derived by something more than chance or chaos. We can reframe our calling to leave behind the roots to flourish.

Here lies a new possibility: a system reset, a deliberate collapse of earthly incentives is something we can strive for. Whether we call it a new epoch or a species level event, creating a new ethos for humanity's spacefaring is a profound challenge. History, journey, exploration, discovery: only a perspective delineates an artefact from a relic. When we design for space, we are designing anthropological infrastructure and archaeological architecture.

Observation at scale along time and distance brings into focus concepts that escape any one momentary vantage point. Our capacity to not only extrapolate allegorical notions of new caves but also juxtapose a theoretical notion of 'what's best' for its occupants is a fascinating proposition. May those in the future never have to ask why notions of capital and lines demarcating an abstract notion of dirt and rock sovereign ownership were not bound when the chance was presented.

Conditions to flourish should be constructed by first removing artefacts of oppression. Interoperability and species exploration run antithetical to money and flags. Occupation and apartheid has been fuelled by inequalities and notions of supremacy; therefore the foundations for exploration to the stars should start with an agreement that humanity will not bring money beyond Mars.

This confluence of economic capacity and territorial sovereignty creates conditions for scarcity. Today, 'new space' companies are building rockets that governments use to carry out scientific exploration. This makes governments dependent on corporations to get to space. This transmission of domain privilege from politics to business changes the incentive structures behind the development of technologies. While governments work to retain their geographical integrity, corporations, on the other hand, are somewhat more ephemeral, as they generally require recapitalizing revenue for solvency.

Our leaders of social and political capita have pioneered the technologies of propulsion, first for national glory and then for corporate profit. Given the financial requirements of space technology, there is little guarantee that any of today's near-space and rocket companies will still be existent entities throughout the entire life cycle of their orbital properties. Defunct, once privately owned space assets could create access denial to space travel for future generations. Furthermore, without a mandated chain of custody, private space companies (and even governments) have little incentive to deal with pressing issues like space debris. We must start demarcating what is to be disassembled and what is to be salvaged, and ensure that orbiting minefields littered with the pieces of their busted satellites do not create a denial of access to our calling of space travel. Opportunity costs of private space ventures can even sometimes outweigh national priorities. The collapse of governments or bankruptcy of companies break a duty of care to see near-Earth assets through their life cycle. A chain of custody to ensure responsible decommissioning must be established as there is virtually no margin of error before a potential catastrophe: a Kessler syndrome event (in which excessive space pollution leads to a high likelihood of collisions) leaving us marooned on Earth.

Future spacecraft will be more than a sum of their technological construction and organic inhabitants; they will be a melting pot of a new type of capsuled clan, and should be adaptable. Beyond principles of interoperability, ontological design and life-sustaining sustainability, they must take into account the full gamut of destructive human capacity. But we can imagine the possibility of an inclusive space age where scarcity is obsolete and the factors that have driven profit and power are mitigated. It can be our calling; a new pursuit of meaning.

With a new pursuit of meaning can come a shared vision for humanity, where commerce and sovereignty is bound together. Nestled in the main asteroid belt between Mars and Jupiter lives Ceres, a dwarf planet.[73] While it's only the 25th largest object in the solar system, Ceres's position – just before the 3AU mark from the Sun (i.e. three times as far from the Sun as Earth) – creates a convenient marker to delineate a socio-cartographic boundary beyond which humanity's

[73]NASA, Ceres Overview. Available from: solarsystem.nasa.gov/planets/dwarf-planets/ceres/overview/

underlying premise changes. To reach the 3AU mark, a craft will have passed Mars, with its furthest point in orbit from the Sun – or its aphelion – at 1.67AU. So if humans dredge capital and capitals with us to space, they should end at Mars; past Ceres, the new set of economic design principles, free of the constraints of terrestrial economics, should begin.

For we are not only the universe observing itself, but part of a cultural quantum qualia and a small piece of the Big Bang pixie dust of neutrinos and anyons that resonate to create a glue holding together boundaries we do not yet comprehend. If there is ever a moment to reframe our perspective of humanity as a continuum, now is that moment.

10

Flying into the Future

By Doug Vining, business and technology futurist and partner at Futureworld

Who needs a flying car? Who can afford one? Do we even want them? And will our cities and airspace ever be ready to accommodate personal air transport? And, if not, what are the alternatives? This article explores the future of urban mobility from drones to driverless cars to reveal what is likely to happen, and what could go wrong.

Since *The Jetsons* cartoons of the 1960s, we've been waiting for that ultimate form of personal mobility, the Flying Car. The idea of being able to avoid traffic and obstacles, and simply zoom off to your destination on autopilot while reading the news or playing board games, captured our imagination for decades, and we all thought it was just a matter of time before this vision of the future became current-day reality.

Well, the future is here, so where's my flying car?

The good news is that they're in development, but they're not cars. Well, the ones that fly aren't cars, but we *are* getting self-driving cars – that don't fly. So, let's dial back a bit, and start there.

For a while now, we've been promised cars that can drive themselves, park themselves, and can be summoned to collect you on demand. In technical terms, this is all possible, but in practical terms, in reality, it's a bit messy. Google's driverless car division, now called Waymo, has very advanced self-driving technology, but you can't buy one. Major auto manufacturers like Ford, BMW, Mercedes[74] and Audi all have advanced autonomous capabilities but no commercial offerings – yet. Audi recently said they would hold off on developing self-driving for the current A8 generation, and although Mercedes have shown off their lounge-like prototype, there's no plan to bring it to market.[75]

Tesla is leading the field with its all-electric vehicles with Autopilot, featuring 'Full Self-Driving' as an (expensive) optional extra, but you still have to keep your hand on the wheel from time to time, and be ready to take over at a moment's notice.

Essentially, the technology is ahead of the regulations, and there's also the simple matter of unpredictable situations. Although the sensors and intelligent systems are capable of safe driving under normal conditions, the computer can't make judgement calls about driving on snow and ice, when lane markings aren't visible, or say, mounting the pavement to avoid an immovable obstacle. But you can take a road trip in a Tesla, and let the car drive itself about 85 per cent of the time, and they'll get better and better.

---

[74]Mercedes-Benz, Daimler AG and BMW Group launch cooperation for automated driving. Available from: www.mercedes-benz.com/en/innovation/daimler-ag-and-bmw-group-launch-cooperation-for-automated-driving/
[75]'Mercedes-Benz ditches self-driving car development', *Driven*, 10 March 2020. Available from: www.driven.co.nz/news/mercedes-benz-ditches-self-driving-car-development/

But a fully driverless car that acts like a robotaxi? We won't have that any time soon, except in structured situations, such as a campus shuttle bus or controlled city centres. It's just too dangerous for auto manufacturers to let the computers decide everything about an unstructured trip, with no manual override.

BUT BACK TO FLYING CARS

That's the promise implicit in any car-sized flying vehicle, that it can fly itself, which is what drones can do. No one expects to become a qualified pilot, just so that you can fly to work or home from the airport. So, the obvious model for a flying car is a passenger drone, or air taxi. That's where it's heading, and there are at least 50 companies[76] working on a variety of concepts and prototypes, some of which have actually flown short distances with one or two people on board.

The original futuristic flying car was the Moller Skycar, which started out as a round, saucer-shaped aircraft with multiple ducted rotors and actually flew a number of times, piloted by Paul Moller himself. His vision for a sleek vehicle that could fit in a garage and fly at speed and altitude was never realized, despite going through several iterations. The primary design flaw was using petrol-powered rotary engines, positioned for forward thrust rather than essential lift. For stability in a craft that can hover and fly vertically, you need fine motor control – in other words, electric motors; like drones.

Most attempts to create a hybrid vehicle that can drive on the road and also fly through the air have resulted in something that is neither a decent car nor a practical plane,

[76]eVTOL Aircraft Directory, Electric VTOL News. Available from: evtol.news/aircraft/

109

such as the Terrafugia Transition, the PAL-V and AeroMobil. In 2009 the American defence research agency DARPA launched the Transformer TX[77] programme, seeking a vehicle capable of driving on land as well as flying into inaccessible places, and able to carry four soldiers. Like a flying Humvee. It failed to produce a viable solution, for the basic reason that any vehicle with robust enough wheels and suspension to traverse ground terrain effectively is too heavy and cumbersome to fly efficiently.

A few of these 'roadable aircraft' models have demonstrated flight, and even announced pre-order availability, but they are not practical personal vehicles, and the transformation from road to air is generally lengthy and complex. Most are unstable in anything but perfect weather.

The latest crop of air taxis and passenger drones has focused purely on being an aircraft; an electric, vertical-take-off-and-landing aircraft. They're not cars.

SO, HOW ARE THEY DOING THEN?

The design challenges all centre around payload, speed, noise and range. Electric motors with multiple rotors are the answer for vertical take-off and landing, and reducing noise, but as long as you're relying on batteries, payload and range are seriously constrained. Batteries are heavy, and run down quickly when you demand maximum power, like take-off and climbing. The more batteries you add to increase range, the more you reduce payload and safety margin for low-power situations. Adding wings and turbo-electric

[77]'Transformer TX', Wikipedia. Available from: en.wikipedia.org/wiki/Aerial_Re-configurable_Embedded_System#Transformer_TX

hybrid engines helps with that, but turbines contribute to increased noise levels. Hydrogen fuel cells represent another option for extending payload and range; fuel cells are costly and technically difficult to deploy, but at least they are quiet.

Recently, in April 2020, the US Air Force upped the ante by launching a programme to accelerate the development of urban aerial vehicles, or 'orbs'. Called 'Agility Prime',[78] this support for the market sees successful operation of commercially developed orbs by 2023. A key player in the development of the supporting networks and infrastructure, rather than the vehicles themselves, is Uber, with their Elevate initiative. Uber sees electric air taxis as the way to extend rides into the third dimension, up into the air, for increased convenience and time-saving, which they call 'productivity'.

Uber is working with at least eight partners at the time of writing, who are all developing air taxis, and will no doubt be looking closely to see who wins under the Agility Prime challenge. In the meantime, their Uber Air division is gaining experience by offering helicopter rides from the airport to New York City. Key to making this a viable service is the ability to pool several passengers in one ride, reducing the individual cost. Achieving scale and integrating air taxis into other modes of urban transport is critical for commercial success. Without commercial levels of adoption and support by customers, the whole idea of passenger drones will remain a 'flying car fantasy' for rich enthusiasts.

As someone who has been watching this space for longer than a decade, I've developed a healthy scepticism for any

[78]Theresa Hitchens, 'Roper Sees Air Force "Flying Cars" In Production by 2023', Breaking Defense, 16 April 2020. Available from: breakingdefense.com/2020/04/roper-sees-air-force-flying-cars-in-production-by-2023/

new flying vehicle that claims convenience, safety and performance, all at once. For example, the EHang 184 was a useful concept, but was never going to be a success as a taxi, carrying only one person in a cramped cockpit. Their 216 model is more promising, but safety is still potentially an issue, if one of the rotors fails.

According to Agility Prime, a key feature of orbs is distributed electric propulsion. In other words, lots of engines and rotors supporting flight. A large number of smaller motors is safer, as the aircraft can continue to fly, or at least land safely, if something fails. Relying on only four points of stability, in a typical quadcopter design, doesn't meet that challenge. Designs with overhead rotors are inherently more stable, having a lower centre of gravity, and gyrodyne configurations, with a large central rotor blade or rotating wing, are probably the safest of all in an emergency, though landing without power under autorotation is decidedly tricky. On the other hand, automated landing, with sufficient power, on a prepared landing zone, is technically simple for current flight software, and demonstrated daily by professional and consumer drones alike. It's not rocket science.

HOW DO WE PICK A WINNER?

The plethora of weird designs and prototypes, from the boat-shaped BlackFly to NEC Corp's hovering skeletal perambulator,[79] is reminiscent of the early days of powered

[79]'NEC unveils flying car prototype using its communications technology', Kyodo News, 5 August 2109. Available from: english.kyodonews.net/news/2019/08/1c-de8723cd37-nec-unveils-flying-car-prototype-using-its-communications-techno-logy.html

flight demonstrated by the Wright brothers. Indeed, one of the projects backed by Larry Page is appropriately called Kitty Hawk. Conversely, Boeing's experimental orb looks just like a light plane with a few rotors[80] stuck on the wings. Bearing in mind that the Wrights first took flight in 1903 and that technology has advanced exponentially since, it's high time aviation was radically reinvented.

It's impossible to say with any confidence which of these concepts and contraptions will become a success, and just like planes and drones, there will probably be a variety of alternatives for different applications. For a general-purpose air taxi, I prefer the idea of a design that incorporates a helicopter-style cabin, with multiple overhead ducted rotors and an auxiliary power source beyond batteries. The Bell Nexus is a likely contender, or perhaps Skai.[81]

And finally, let's not ignore how motor racing has helped give birth to important innovations for cars, both in safety and performance. The Formula 1 World Championship in particular has been the breeding ground for all sorts of inventions and improvements, from turbochargers to anti-lock braking, many of which are simply taken for granted in a modern 'sensible' car. Now we can take this innovation model into the air. Airspeeder[82] wants to

---

[80] Anurag Kotoky and Julie Johnsson, 'Boeing's Flying Car Has Taken Off', Bloomberg, 23 January 2019. Available from: www.bloomberg.com/news/articles/2019-01-23/boeing-s-flying-car-takes-off-to-show-a-glimpse-of-the-future

[81] Jessica Miley, 'Look to the "Skai": The Future of Flying Vehicles is Here', Interesting Engineering, 1 June 2019. Available from: interestingengineering.com/look-to-the-skai-the-future-of-flying-vehicles-is-here

[82] 'Airspeeder is Motorsport Evolved', Airspeeder. Available from: airspeeder.com/about

reinvent racing around a track by putting it above the ground – like Formula 1, but airborne. It looks exciting, but daredevil stuff!

WHAT ABOUT THE MARKET?

Google's parent Alphabet estimates the market for passenger drones in 2035 as US$32 billion, and for cargo or goods delivery drones, around US$4 billion. These estimates are highly speculative, and depend entirely on the development of infrastructure and business models, as well as the vehicles themselves, air traffic technology and regulatory approvals. These developments are years, if not decades, away.

As Alphabet's blog points out,[83] the high cost of transportation drones favours usership rather than ownership, and once commercialization begins, even network operators like Uber will rely on either manufacturers or specialist leasing companies to provide and maintain their fleet. Large companies with multiple urban locations that can economically support an air shuttle service would similarly outsource fleet operations to specialist providers, while the market for individual ownership of these aircraft would be negligible.

Elon Musk, who often seems to be able to make the seemingly impossible happen, has gone on record as saying that flying cars are definitely not the future of transport. I agree with him entirely. Flying *cars* are not the future. But when it comes to air taxis and orbs, there is definitely a future I can imagine, where these electric aircraft are part of the

---

[83]Claudia Bauer and Twan van den Elsen, 'Passenger drone technology and flying cars', Alphabet, 16 April 2019. Available from: www.alphabet.com/en-ww/blog/passenger-drone-technology-and-flying-cars

way we get around cities. If it's possible to make electric cars affordable mainstream vehicles, and to routinely land reusable space rockets back at the launch pad, then, in the future, it must be possible to take a ride in a passenger drone, without having to be a mad scientist.

Whether you call them orbs or passenger drones or air taxis, these flying machines are redefining the future of urban mobility. The future starts now; let's get going!

PART THREE

(In)human Capital

The bad news is, the robots are coming.

Experts expect that anywhere between 20 per cent and 50 per cent of jobs worldwide are at some risk of replacement by technology in the 21st century.

Now, those are some scary statistics, especially given the world's already precarious inequality levels – if taken at face value. However, it should be pointed out that, even if those worst-case figures are correct (and, as with anything when it comes to the future, that is highly unlikely), they reflect gross job replacement due to automation, not net jobs lost to automation.

As much as there will be employees displaced and human jobs replaced by artificial intelligence and automation in the coming years (and we should absolutely not forget about those left behind), there will also be new – as yet unimagined – jobs created. Even if the new jobs created due to technological developments are not as numerous as the jobs lost due to technological efficiencies, the automation 'job apocalypse' is likely not *quite* as dire as the scaremongers would have us believe.

For one thing, we also need to understand that even the employees adversely affected by automation are also themselves consumers who are benefiting from the same efficiencies that may have cost them their jobs. Advances in technological automation have given, and will continue to give, consumers increasing cost and convenience benefits as what were once upper-middle-class luxuries – such as internet connectivity, access to global air travel, and educational content from top-tier universities which are becoming available – to even the poorest strata of society as Wi-Fi and data costs tend towards zero. Of course, this does not put food on the table in the short term, but it does provide individuals with access to practical tools, knowledge, and opportunities to re-skill themselves to earn a living in a new career.

For another, we need to separate our understanding of what jobs and work are. Jobs are something you do for a boss in exchange for a salary. Work is something you do for yourself on your own terms. *Jobs* that exchange a fixed amount of time for a fixed income are a relic of the industrial era that is rapidly being replaced by *work* that exchanges results for value. With jobs, the terms are defined up front: job workers exchange potential upside for the security of protecting their downside exposure. Work is the opposite – it allows us to share in unlimited upside, which trades off against potential downside risk. Whichever way you look at it, though, the world is headed towards a place where work, with reciprocal up- and downside skin in the game, replaces the illusion of safety and security of a salary (we say 'the illusion of', because the average half-life of a large listed company is around 10 per cent of what they were 100 years ago). Furthermore, big companies are more likely to work in automatable industries, and more likely to invest in automation initiatives than smaller (more human) firms. In other words, looking ahead, salaried workers will be *more* vulnerable than the gainfully self-employed. And that could actually be something to celebrate.

We are worth more than a minimum living wage in a dead-end job. We need to find a way to add value to each other, in life-affirming value-creating work, rather than slogging away in a poorly paying job that offers us nothing more than a salary and the distant promise of 'retirement' once we are all worn out and used up.

That said, change is painful. The fact remains that many, many people will have to switch careers (often more than once) in order to survive in a world that increasingly appears to treat flesh-and-blood human beings as assets rather than individuals. And human beings are not mere 'collateral damage' – financial stability and at least the reasonable expectation of the *opportunity* for personal progress is essential for a safe, prosperous society.

In order to minimize disruptive human job losses and financial pain, as we shift from the world of comfortable (if unfulfilling) jobs to the insecure (yet freeing) world of work, and maximize the benefits from new technologies, we need to ensure we are adequately skilled for the work that *will* be around in the future.

The good news is the jobs and job functions most at risk are the jobs hardly anyone actually enjoys doing anyway.

Routine, process-driven jobs – both professional and entry level – are at the most risk of automation by a robot or algorithm. This is why professional accountants and paralegals now find themselves in the same boat that blue-collar factory, farm and mineworkers found themselves in during the 20th century. As such, 21st-century knowledge and worker skills (yes, even many university degrees) will no longer be a guarantee against technological redundancy.

Of course, not all human skills are destined to become redundant. In fact, the most human skills – high-touch skills, particularly those involving *creativity* and interpersonal *connection* (which are also more fun than rote job functions), are of the highest value to the workers, customers and employers. After all, as long as we have warm human bodies, those warm human bodies have irrational (very human) needs and desires that can only be fulfilled by our fellow human creators.

And that is, of course, the key: work that adds value to fellow human beings' lives will always be in demand.

The trick is to understand that the future of work is changing and that the jobs we do tomorrow will be very different to the jobs we do today. This means we need to prepare ourselves for a future filled with learning, development and change (ah, that endless change!). And that means that the most important future-proof skill to develop is the ability to learn (and relearn), rather than learned knowledge in and of itself.

This of course means that our stale old education system also needs to be reinvented, from pearly childhood development right through to lifelong adult learning (Andrew Vorster's chapter goes into that whole journey in much greater detail).

By committing to a lifetime of continual reskilling and upskilling, and by ensuring that we differentiate between jobs best done by machines and work best done by humans, we can work together to design a future where technology assists humans in living more fulfilling, more rewarding lives, rather than making humans redundant.

Overall, if we wish to maximize productivity for organizations and maximize happiness and life satisfaction for human beings, we need to distinguish between robot tasks and human tasks. Automating cost centres and dead-end jobs that do not offer human workers satisfaction in their work makes complete sense, and should indeed be fast-tracked, not merely to maximize profits, but rather to free the millions of very human workers around the world currently trapped in dead-end, very inhuman jobs. Likewise, humanizing value-adding and essential service functions also makes good business – and good social – sense. Leave robot tasks to the bots and human roles to the people.

In this section, (In)human Capital, our authors look at how we can retain and reclaim our humanity, sanity and productivity in the age of machines – in an inclusive and collaborative way, rather than succumbing to the exploitative and exclusionary view of insiders versus outsiders.

As you read these chapters, we encourage you to ask yourself the tough yet essential questions:

Are you, personally, in a value-creating role in your company? Or are you a cost centre?

Is your business in the business of value creation or value extraction?

Does your industry build and make or does it merely collect rents and tolls from those who do?

Are you leaving behind more than you are taking from the system?

11

The Future of Education

by Andrew Vorster, an innovation consultant, futurist, speaker and writer

The 'teachers in classrooms'-based education system has been broken for generations, yet we keep trying to make it work, churning out students fit for an industrial age long past, without equipping them for the future. We 'educate' to the lowest common denominator in the class; we see technology as something to interact with as opposed to integrate into customized learning journeys to educate each child individually to bring out the best of their natural ability. In this chapter we look at how technology can and should make us better humans, rather than mould us into its own robotic image.

As I'm sure is the case with siblings all over the world, my older sister and I will occasionally get into a heated argument where neither of us is willing to back down and the only resolution is to agree to disagree.

Such is the case on the topic of The Future of Education.

For background context, I'm in my fifties and have spent my life driving innovation, change and transformation across multiple industries in numerous geographies across the world and hopefully will continue to do so for the next 40 years or so. Yes, you read that right – I'm under no illusion when it comes to my (lack of) ability to retire and I have no desire to anyway – I'll be ~~causing trouble~~ innovating until I drop dead.

My sister is in her sixties and is a teacher. She is one of those truly passionate people who felt 'called' into teaching from an early age, attended teaching college straight out of school and has been educating kids ever since.

In my personal opinion, the current system of formal school-based education up to the age of approximately 18 years that is followed in many countries across the world is fundamentally broken.

Before you put down this book in anger and dive for the keyboard to flame me on social media, I'll outline a few reasons why I've been developing this belief for many years and how the COVID-19 crisis has brought many of these points into sharp focus by challenging previous assumptions that have been widely accepted.

'SCHOOL IS A PLACE YOU GO TO GET EDUCATED'

I start with this point, as it was one of the first impacts of lockdown felt by parents. Schools closed and children were sent home – how could they possibly learn if they weren't 'going to school'? Did parents now suddenly have to become teachers in order to home-school their kids? (Many tried bravely, and some were no doubt pretty successful – more on this later.)

I used to have frequent arguments with my father as he would ask me why I wasn't 'going to work' every day when I was working remotely. I used to tell him 'work is something I do, NOT a place I go', but he couldn't get his head around the fact that I could work from anywhere, so long as I had an internet connection and my laptop. To him, I was just 'playing on my computer' and until the day he died he thought work was somewhere you went every day.

Millions of people around the world have been working entirely remotely for the last few decades and suddenly millions more became part of 'the world's biggest remote working Proof of Concept (PoC)' due to COVID. Eyes have been opened to the fact that millions of people don't have to 'go to work (in a physical place) every day' and that they can quite happily do their jobs remotely, quite often more efficiently and most definitely with less of an impact to their health, well-being, and disposable income due to the lack of commuting.

So how is 'going to school' any different?

Do children have to go to (a physical) school in order to get educated?

Well, of course not.

There are approximately 1.7 million children being home-schooled in the US alone.[84] Many of these will have been home-schooled by parents but many others would have been attending online classes delivered by a teacher or been engaged in self-paced offline or online learning.

---

[84]Brian D. Ray, 'Homeschooling Growing: Multiple Data Points Show Increase 2012 to 2016 and Later', NHERI, 20 April 2018. Available from: www.nheri.org/homeschool-population-size-growing/

COVID-19, of course, had a massive impact on schools globally, with the World Economic Forum (WEF) reporting that 1.2 BILLION children were out of classrooms due to school closures.[85] The article went on to say that the Chinese government instructed a quarter of a billion full-time students to resume their classes online and as the lockdowns spread across the planet, more and more countries followed suit.

As part of my research for this article (yes, I don't just make this stuff up), I interviewed 12-year-old Arsam Matin, aka 'Arsam Futurist',[86] the self-described youngest member of the World Futures Studies Federation (WFSF) and co-founder of Gen Z Futurists. Arsam was born in Iran in 2008 and became a refugee at age seven. He now lives in Kurdistan with his mother (Mina) and stepfather (Dana).

Despite never setting foot in school for a single day of his life so far (except to deliver presentations to schoolchildren), Arsam speaks three languages fluently and is currently learning a fourth. He is incredibly articulate in English, a language he taught himself by playing games online and watching television with English subtitles. Arsam grew up without a father and while his mother taught him the basics of reading and writing in his early years, the bulk of his education was via a slow internet connection and an ageing tablet.

When Dana (who has a Masters in English and previously taught it for 12 years) met Arsam for the first time a few years ago, he was astonished at his level of accomplishment and, by his assessment, Arsam exceeded the academic abilities of

[85]Cathi Li and Farah Lalani, 'The COVID-19 pandemic has changed education forever. This is how', World Economic Forum, 29 April 2020. Available from: www.weforum.org/agenda/2020/04/coronavirus-education-global-covid19-online-digit-al-learning

[86]Generation Z Futurists. Available from: genzfuturists.com/

most children his age when assessed by traditional means. As a long-standing member of the WFSF, Dana introduced Arsam to the concept of futures studies, nurturing his passion for personal learning and development, which has developed into a deep desire to create a way to completely disrupt current formal education by democratizing access to knowledge globally.

That's quite an ambition for a kid that's never 'been to school'.

UNESCO also updated its distance learning guide[87] for the children that were affected by school closures and provided links to a raft of resources, including national learning portals and digital education tools, to support the continuation of learning during lockdown. In many parts of the world, teachers moved from physical to digital spaces and lessons resumed, almost as they were before.

Suddenly, it became apparent to many more people that school did not necessarily need to be a place you physically go – causing many to consider a new way of educating their children going forward as part of their personal 'new normal'.

Of course, this model doesn't work for everyone and there are some major issues that were uncovered by children no longer having a physical place to go to every day to learn, e.g.:

- Many were excluded from online learning due to lack of access to digital resources – particularly (but not limited to) developing nations and rural communities;[88]

[87]UNESCO, 2020. COVID-19, 'Education: From disruption to recovery'. Available from: en.unesco.org/covid19/educationresponse
[88]UK Government, 'New major package to support online learning', 19 April 2020. Available from: www.gov.uk/government/news/new-major-package-to-support-on-line-learning

- Millions of children missed out on the only meal of the day that had previously been provided at school;[89]
- For many children, school has been a sanctuary outside an abusive home;
- Many parents had jobs that required them to be out of the house, and so sending their kids to a physical space to go to school was the only way they could remain employed, safe in the knowledge that their children were in somebody else's care.

In my opinion, these are largely societal issues, which can and should be addressed in ways other than sending children to (a physical) school.

The major issues highlighted by the sudden transition to remote schooling were not directly related to the effectiveness of the current classroom-based school system. Indeed, the same WEF report previously mentioned indicates that online learning might well be better than classroom-based learning. The report states that, on average, students retain 25–60 per cent more material from online compared to classroom learning, mainly because online learning, which allows students to self-pace and self-direct their learning journeys, ends up reducing learning times by 40–60 per cent compared to traditional classroom settings.

So far, none of what I've said above unequivocally supports my position that the current system of schooling is fundamentally broken and, in fact, it tends to indicate that this system is fine but could be modernized, perhaps simply

[89]UK Government, 'Providing free school meals during the coronavirus (COVID-19) outbreak', Guidance For Schools, updated 15 July 2020. Available from: www.gov.uk/government/publications/covid-19-free-school-meals-guidance/covid-19-free-school-meals-guidance-for-schools

'digitized' in order to cater for the future – so I'm going to be a bit more provocative with the next assumption that was challenged by recent events.

'THE WAY IT'S ALWAYS BEEN'

The (predominantly Western) schooling system hasn't had a fundamental revamp since the 1800s. Sure, the curricula have changed (not as radically as you might expect) and we have a few more exotic subjects available for study than back then, but the fundamental approach in the majority of mainstream schools is exactly the same as it was all those years ago.

Teachers teach what they have been taught via a curriculum that is taught at the pace of the slowest learner in the class in a 'one-size-fits-all' approach.

The way that academic progress is assessed hasn't changed much either. The system of tests and exams favours 'memory over mastery' of a topic, which has no bearing on adult life after school.

There are exceptions to the rule and other teaching methodologies, such as Montessori,[90] Waldorf,[91] Harkness,[92] Sudbury[93] and Reggio Emilia.[94] I am personally a huge fan of the Montessori approach, which is very 'child-centric', and both of our children attended Montessori schools in their

[90]Montessori, Montessori Method. Available from: www.montessori.org.uk/about-us/what-is-montessori

[91]Waldorf, Waldorf Method. Available from: waldorfanswers.org/Waldorf.htm

[92]Harkness, Harkness Method. Available from: www.beds.ac.uk/jpd/volume-4-issue-3/harkness-learning-principles-of-a-radical-american-pedagogy/

[93]Sudbury, Sudbury Method. Available from: hvsudburyschool.com/the-sudbury-model-of-education/

[94]Reggio, Reggio Amilia Method. Available from: www.reggiochildren.it/en/reggio-emilia-approach/

early years. But I'm talking mainstream, primarily (Western) government/state schools that cater to the masses – there is little opportunity for a teacher to do anything outside what the curriculum and evaluation system dictates.

We, and most of our children, have been subject to a school system born out of the industrial age, where the intention was to provide a standardized level of education in order for people to be employable and to give potential employers a means of assessing their employability (via the results of standardized tests).

The World Economic Forum (WEF) stated in 2016 that according to popular estimates, 65 per cent of children entering primary education will be entering jobs that haven't been invented yet[95] ... how on earth can we expect an antiquated educational system to prepare us for the future?

Which brings me on to an interesting question on the survey I ran as further research for this chapter. While the relatively low number of responses mean that this survey is not 'statistically significant', the responses nonetheless provide interesting insights.

I asked:

'What do you think the primary purpose of a structured education should be?'

The available responses were:

1 Basic academic skills and the discipline of learning
2 Expand creativity and independent thinking

[95]'The Future of Jobs and Skills', World Economic Forum, 2016. Available from: reports.weforum.org/future-of-jobs-2016/chapter-1-the-future-of-jobs-and-skills/

3 Enable each child to unlock their own unique potential
4 Prepare for life as an adult
5 Other (open text response)

Out of those adults who had already completed formal education (including parents), 76.5 per cent said 'Enable each child to unlock their own unique potential' and 17.6 per cent said 'Expand creativity and independent thinking'.

This was in stark contrast to the responses from educators, where 40 per cent answered 'Enable each child to unlock their own unique potential' and another 40 per cent said 'Prepare for life as an adult'.

While adults overwhelmingly expect educators to unlock the potential of each child individually, the reality is that this isn't generally possible in a group classroom setting where everyone follows the same curriculum at the same time of the day, and it is even more difficult in large classes.

What was even more interesting was the responses to the follow-on question to this, where I asked:

'Are you satisfied that the current education system adequately prepares children for adult life and work?'

To this question, 94.4 per cent of adults and 66.7 per cent of educators responded 'NO'.

So if the majority of us (educators included) don't think that school adequately prepares children for adult life and educators are unable to unlock every child's unique potential in a classroom-based setting, why are we continuing to send our kids to school?

Surely there is a better way?

The 2020 lockdown caused widespread panic among many parents who, as they attempted to replicate the role of their children's teachers, were desperately trying to recall junior school geography and high school algebra lessons in order to keep their kids busy with worksheets sent home by schools.

What many quickly discovered is that everyday life itself presents many different learning opportunities and not all that is learned by children is taught by a schoolteacher or learned in a classroom. In fact, there is quite a bit specifically NOT taught at school in which parents should perhaps be taking more of an active role in teaching their kids – like how to prepare a budget, which also came into sharp focus during lockdown as millions of people all over the world found themselves with reduced or no income for an extended period of time.

Another question I asked was:

'Do you (or did you) encourage or teach your children to learn skills not taught at school?'

On this front, 84.6 per cent of adults had indeed done so via a mix of approaches, including teaching their children themselves, leading by example, positive parenting, engaging specialist tutors, enabling life experiences and encouraging topic exploration and hobbies; and of course the Internet played a huge part, with online courses and YouTube featuring heavily in examples given.

Since it was an online survey where respondents were contacted via social media, the heavy influence of digital tools is to be expected. In fact, 86.7 per cent of respondents had themselves learned skills not taught at school (or university) so it is unsurprising that this same cohort would encourage their children to do the same.

'POSSIBLE, PLAUSIBLE, PROBABLE AND PREFERRED FUTURES'

Astonishingly, 66.7 per cent of the respondents to my survey answered 'YES' to the question:

'Do you think children will still "go to school" 100 years from now?'

I had thought (hoped) that setting a date in the far future would ignite people's imagination and get them thinking about 'the art of the possible', but it seems that despite deep dissatisfaction with the current system, the majority of people simply cannot imagine a future without school as we know it today (my sister, of course, being one of those!).

My personal opinion is somewhat different and is more aligned with the 33.3 per cent of respondents who answered 'NO'.

My preferred future leans heavily on the (distant) past.

In Ancient Rome, those that could afford it would engage the services of private tutors and 'masters' of their craft to mentor their children in a wide spectrum of topics, ranging from art and science to politics and economics. India had the Gurukula system, where anyone who wished to study approached a teacher (guru) and, if they were accepted, then they would live with them for a period of time until they had learned what they wanted or until the guru believed they had nothing more to teach the student. Similar constructs can be found across all ancient civilizations, and the common thread is that education was 'child-led' at their pace and in their areas of interest.

Today, almost all of humanity's accumulated knowledge is available on the Internet and access to 'masters' and mentors in every subject imaginable is (often free and) merely a click away for those who have access to technology.

There is a rapidly evolving 'app store approach' to education on the horizon. One where we can pick and choose our subjects and interests from multiple different 'schools' and educators and assemble them with the same ease as customizing our mobile phone options according to our individual preferences.

We could, if we choose to, use this capability to guide our children (and ourselves) to truly unlock each person's individual potential in a way that current school structures and curricula simply cannot.

This is my personal preferred future, one that is technologically augmented, enabled and accelerated.

One where we are all both students and teachers at the same time.

It is the very heart of the argument where my sister and I agree to disagree (for now).

12

The Psychology of Teams

*by Duena Blomstrom, keynote speaker, author,
co-founder and CEO of Emotional Banking™
and PeopleNotTech Ltd.™*

We need to put humans back in charge of business. After
all, we – ourselves, our employers, our employees, our
suppliers and our customers – are all warm-bodied humans.
It is important to remember businesses are built for and by
people – even in the increasingly automated economy we
find ourselves in. We need to redefine the concept of 'team'
itself to reflect the human side of the companies we build
and keep. This chapter explores the possibilities for a more
human-centric future of work.

For the past 30 years, there has been an ongoing discussion
on the ways in which work will evolve in the future. As we all
recognized, we can no longer keep working in the same way
as we have since the Industrial Revolution.

The common understanding was that much needed
to change – I coined the term 'Human Debt'™ (akin to
the term 'tech debt'), which refers to the efforts required

for employees to be happy and productive at work. In essence, the model in which we would all go to our offices to perform traditional jobs in commonly accepted ways – effectively punching in and out as if it were 1985 – is obviously not sustainable.

There are two primary reasons behind this lack of sustainability: the speed of technology and the expectations of digital consumers. In other words, given how fast we have to employ technology to produce products and services at the speed and quality that consumers expect, the old ways of work have become unfeasible. Everything, from how we employ new workers to the working conditions we provide for them, is poised for extreme change.

Indeed, this change had started to be evident in some segments of the knowledge industry such as software development, where their ways of work had to adapt to fit with the advent of new processes, such as the implementation of Lean theories or Agile practices.

A high concentration of these new ways of working emerged in Silicon Valley, within companies who are showing great success (such as Amazon or Google, who are famously able to efficiently implement new features and remain ahead of their competition), while the rest of the world was slowly starting to take notice and reconsider the ways in which they viewed traditional concepts and conventions of work, when dismissing these outdated approaches seemed to be so efficient for these winners.

We can refer to these winners as the 'Digital Elite', a term used in technology reports to designate the type of company that is consistently over-performing and has high degrees of productivity. They all seem to have a lot in common, and most of these commonalities have to do with their extreme focus on people instead of process and their willingness to redefine work in whatever way suits their business goals.

Granted, being digitally native companies gives GAFA (Google, Apple, Facebook and Amazon) and others an almost unfair advantage, but even the most traditional businesses could make changes that would propel them into the 'digital elite' category should they truly desire to do so. Reports and statistics finally started to make their way into boardrooms to highlight the importance of placing humans at the centre of their operations and, as a result, they are starting to usher in more transformations and change programmes to reflect the new ways of working and new innovative ideas.

Now, most conversations regarding the future of work revolved almost exclusively around the idea of 'the culture of the organization', which, while providing a lot of fodder for lyricizing, is far from having any semblance of practical application and really should be universally replaced with actionable elements – the individual, the work and the team.

The latter of these three is, in my view, the most important element of them all. The team. Over the past years the team has gone from revered to all but abandoned, yet it remains the most potent element and representation of human interaction at work.

QUESTION EVERYTHING

The reality is that while our core structures are the same ones that were developed by the work environments of the 80s (or even the 60s, in some cases), we are now finding ourselves in a completely new paradigm in which rigid groups who operate and communicate through antiquated methods are asked to work in ways that will bring GAFA-like agility – and that simply is not possible. The best practice of the process before was systematic, linear and slow. Today it is flexible, agile and extremely fast.

So what should we question and ultimately change if we truly want the innovation and speed of success that the future of work should bring us?

THE 'WHERE'

The main assumption worth challenging is 'open-plan offices rule!' This mentality remains prominent, despite the fact that it has been scientifically debunked by study after study, such as Ethan Bernstein and Stephen Turban's 2018 Harvard-commissioned 'The impact of the "open" workspace on human collaboration'[96] and others, showing that open-plan offices create toxic workplaces, uncollaborative environments and reduced productivity – and employees hate them.

In this debate, the idea of the futility of the office itself – because so many tasks could be performed from home computers, or anywhere at all – wasn't given serious consideration; it was largely treated as mere fodder for after-hours conversations or a theme for exclusively theoretical debates. Yet this is where the debate should really lie – do we need office space at all?

THE 'WHEN'

The idea of flexibility in terms of schedule is not new, but it has been lumped in with the topic of remote working and buried at the bottom of the drawer. It has been mired with the fear

[96]https://royalsocietypublishing.org/doi/10.1098/rstb.2017.0239

of possible toxicity from employees who are uninvested in the company's productivity, leading to the view that it merely widens the opportunity for procrastination and inactivity. Yet surveys such as 'People and the Bottom Line' (2018, Institute for Employment Studies and The Work Foundation),[97] and 'The future of work: jobs and skills in 2030' (2014, UKCES)[98] show that employees who are allowed to work flexibly become immensely more productive and engaged than their overly scheduled colleagues.

Ideas around flexible work are not new, with experiments around four-day working weeks having been successfully run in New Zealand and Scandinavia and with freelancers everywhere having optimized the ways that they apply themselves to their body of work, giving rise to the phenomenon of digital nomads – people who travel and live wherever they choose, while relying on digital technology to make a living; and firms such as Ryan Accounting have seen spectacular results after implementing a completely flexible working policy with no hours or specific location demands. But such isolated instances never found their way into the mainstream discourse pre-pandemic.

Likely, over the next few years, we will finally rely on technology to empower office work and use data intelligently enough to understand productivity patterns and match them exactly to the needs of individual teams. If we start understanding the 'golden time' of scintillating productivity

[97]P. Tamkin, M. Cowling, W. Hunt (2008), 'People and the Bottom Line', Institute for Employment Studies. Available at: https://www.employment-studies.co.uk/system/files/resources/files/448.pdf
[98]P. Tamkin, M. Cowling, W. Hunt (2008), 'People and the Bottom Line', Institute for Employment Studies. Available at: https://www.employment-studies.co.uk/system/files/resources/files/448.pdf

that each employee has, then we can start harmonizing this for the most effective teamwork while also allowing individual contributions to take place whenever and wherever the person is truly most productive, even if it's in the middle of the night while nursing their baby or in the early mornings at Starbucks.

In other words, work has become truly flexible, and we could have had it this way all along – before inflexibility stopped being achievable as a result of the pandemic.

THE 'HOW'

Ways of working, processes and tools. A hot topic before the pandemic, with its incarnations ranging from how the 'digital elite' did things all the way down to the companies who pretended they had never heard of the terms 'digital transformation' or 'agile', with the vast majority of companies stuck in a middle ground, where they had invariably started on some form of change towards implementing new ways of working.

Even if we overlook the trendy terms, some common elements of this new paradigm are clear across the board – we all know that we need communication tools to stay in touch, and programming tools to develop software, but we're not entirely sure which ones work best and what method of mixing and matching them gives us the best results. But are we asking the right questions? How many organizations have audited the need for various legacy systems? Who wondered if they really need a Customer Relationship Management (CRM) system? Who checked if they should even have time sheets? Who split their company in two so they A/B test the introduction of Scrum? Most importantly, which of these organizations have placed enough emphasis on creating a human practice to augment the technical capability that they have offered their employees?

In the absence of true organizational design and of a deep understanding of the new ways of working and how each would fit each enterprise culture, many of these 'transformations' to new ways of working won't prove successful.

THE 'WHY': WHERE IS THE HEART?

Why do we work and why should we care about work? By looking at successful enterprises, we now know work isn't just to pay the bills, which is only the base of the pyramid. The complexity of human motivation transcends solely monetary incentives, so we should commit ourselves to finding a greater purpose.

There is a famous anecdote about when JFK asked a NASA janitor 'What do you do here?' and he responded with 'I help put a man on the moon'. This illustrates shared purpose – the magic of having every single soul in the organization believe in the same mission and goals.

This shared purpose is obviously valuable, but so hard to attain across the board. For leaders, being invested enough to earnestly want the company to succeed requires enough courage and emotional quotient (EQ) as to be willing to do whatever it takes – whether that is raising uncomfortable questions or taking flexibility to heart. This could be something as small as allowing people to come in late after a dental appointment or maybe even letting an employee work from a jungle village – allowing them to replicate a Kanban board with coconut shells, as long as they have Wi-Fi and a willingness to apply their skills and their hearts to the project!

Creating a 'people practice' and investing in the EQ of leadership will also help us here – we would be able to comprehend what makes people tick and they will, in turn, become emotionally invested in their company, in what they are collectively trying to achieve and why.

THE 'WHO': TEAMS AND INDIVIDUALS

Let's look at our greatest capital – the humans in the organization. In particular, let's consider the difference between individuals and teams and how we need to become genuinely obsessed with both of these elements.

First, it is no secret that the way people become part of a team today in the context of organizations is highly coincidental – based on a combination of availability, keywords on a spreadsheet and anecdotal evidence at best. For all the studies that show that the dynamic of a team is crucial to its success, and for all the evidence showing that emotionally intelligent and highly engaged team members produce the best results the fastest, little has been done to apply such studies to everyday work. That is chiefly because, while they know on paper how important they are, business leaders often have no clue who their employees really are or what they really think and feel.

Office workers are often left incredibly unscrutinized and soon become aware of this – leading them to feel justifiably alienated and undervalued as a result.

If you pick up a book by modern thought leaders such as Brené Brown or Patty McCord, you'll find they all agree that there is a severe lack of serious feedback on the part of the employees. They all bemoan the farce that is a yearly survey in a world that moves at breakneck speed and they encourage leaders to ask questions incessantly.

Once we shift the focus away from the nebulous term of 'the culture of the organization' and towards the actionable elements of the humans and the teams they operate in, and we start asking them caring and curious questions from a place of high EQ, we can start working on the 'human debt' and stop working in the same way we have done since the Industrial Revolution.

THE MAGIC: WHAT MAKES SOME TEAMS ELITE?

Of all the unexamined topics above, maybe the one that hurts us most in its absence is: what makes a team tick? How come some teams are amazing together and perform to the height of their abilities delivering astounding results, whereas most just toddle along?

This has been the driving force behind a cross-team four-year-long major study of the impact of diversity on 180 teams in Google – understanding how their magic happens. Having started with the assumption that it had to do with the composition of the team – i.e. what individuals were part of it – they had to concede at the end of surveying 50,000 employees and analysing over 100 co-ordinates that the data indicated that 'psychological safety' was the major determinant of team efficiency.

'Individuals on teams with higher psychological safety are less likely to leave Google, they're more likely[99] to harness the power of diverse ideas[100] from their teammates, they

[99] 'Why diversity matters', McKinsey, 1 January 2015. Available from: www.mckinsey.com/business-functions/organization/our-insights/why-diversity-matters
[100] Joann S. Lublin, 'New Report Finds a "Diversity Dividend" at Work', *Wall Street Journal*, 20 January 2015. Available from: blogs.wsj.com/atwork/2015/01/20/new-report-finds-a-diversity-dividend-at-work/

bring in more revenue, and they're rated as effective twice as often by executives.'

Coined by academics in the 1960s, the term 'psychological safety' was researched further and popularized in the 1990s by Harvard's Professor Dr Amy Edmondson. It is loosely defined as 'a team's shared belief that they are safe for taking intrapersonal risks and therefore speak up, innovate and create good results together in a family-like structure'. Professor Dr Edmondson observed it at play in the medical and aviation industries among others, where it correlated not only to business results but also to patient or passenger safety – as a lack of communication and collaboration often had disastrous consequences.

Following Google's findings, the term was thrust into the mainstream and it became even more important once it started being analysed and recognized as the only indicator of performance in organizational teams in the knowledge industry (and particularly in software companies).

10 STEPS TO REDUCE YOUR 'HUMAN DEBT' AND BUILD A FUTURE-PROOF WORK ORGANIZATION

1 **Question every existent work stereotype**. Where you can and it makes more sense for your organization – redesign from scratch and throw conventional wisdom and unexamined precedents out the window.

2 **Ask! Ask! Ask!** Make true, honest and frequent feedback a priority and ensure a curious and open-hearted channel exists that your employees believe in.

3 **Stop measuring input and start measuring output**. Flexible and remote working will follow as the logical

conclusion of this. Where and how people do the work is not what matters.

4 **Obsess about the team and the humans.** Build a 'people practice' in both yourself and any other managers in the enterprise. Realize that they no longer have any more important 'day job' than that of understanding and catering for their team's needs.

5 **Increase the leaders' EQ.** Most of the leaders of teams have never had to rely on their emotional intelligence in the workplace before. Many can't even recognize and address basic emotions in their team.

6 **Make psychological safety the number 1 priority.** When we have a clear lever for betterment such as psychological safety, which ensures people are open and honest, curious and engaged, don't choose to refrain from opinion out of fear. Instead, learn and innovate together – we must make it an extreme priority and ensure it is always kept front of mind.

7 **Let go of command and control.** The idea of keeping everyone in check by a combination between process and micro-management doesn't yield the results we want and it's now clear that autonomous, entrepreneurial teams are so much more productive. Adopting servile leadership – where leaders are only there to remove blockers from the pathway of psychologically safe, independent teams that make magic together – should be paramount.

8 **Give everyone permission to be human.** For too long at work, emotions were a dirty word. It has been seen as 'unprofessional' to even mention them, let alone show them at work. We were expected to leave them at the door. This has created most of the

'human debt' – if we want high performance, we must encourage people to bring their whole, authentic, intensely human and therefore emotion-driven selves to work.

9 **Adopt the new ways of working in ways that make the most sense to your organization.** Don't blindly follow a prescriptive framework but design the methods and ways that make the best sense to you. Most of all, be prepared to change them often and on the dime.

10 **Focus on changing ways of thinking to become truly #FitForVUCA.** We are living in unprecedented times and everything is in flux. This is uncomfortable and unsettling to most if not all of us, but we must remain obstinately anchored in our resilience and flexibility and therefore be agile at heart and ready to face whatever challenges are ahead when we have strong teams around us.

Looking ahead, the only certainty we have is that we need to focus on the one most effective unit of work: the team and creating a people practice to help it flourish. Ultimately, if we stay firmly focused on EQed humans in psychologically safe teams, we stand a chance of remaining highly performant irrespective of what the future demands of work prove to be.

13

We Welcome Our New Robot Overlords

by Theo Priestley, anti-futurist, technologist and keynote speaker

No, robots are not going to take your job, but they may take your life… So can humans live alongside robots, robot rights and killer robots? In this essay we explore how organizations can prepare for a cultural revolution in accepting robot co-workers, robo-bosses and even robocops. We also address the requirements for building a future with robotic co-existence at every level of society; the threat of a 'super AI'; and what we can do to prevent the robots we made to help us from inadvertently destroying us.

Whenever someone talks about artificial intelligence, the immediate reaction is to conjure an image of something in robotic form with glowing eyes and, more often than not, it's eviscerating humans with some kind of futuristic weaponry. Popularized by science fiction movies, both seem to go hand in hand when in truth it is sadly rather boring and mundane and there is very little need to have, for example, a Boston Dynamics' Atlas staring down the boardroom table dressed in a Hugo Boss suit and waving a PowerPoint deck.

However, the idea that an invisible entity can hold a seat with the rest of the executive leadership and play an active role in driving company vision and performance is no longer as fantastical as it sounds, and more and more recognized figures are coming forward with predictions to testify that the enterprise boardroom faces a rather messy shake-up in the near future.

Jack Ma, the (former) chairman and CEO of Alibaba, famously opined in 2017 that he expected to see an AI on the cover of *Time* magazine as 'CEO of the Year' within the next 30 years. In itself, the notion of a robotic AI leading a company even within the next century is both exciting and unsettling for many as it drives home just how fast technology appears to be advancing today.

> Thirty years later, the *Time* magazine cover for the best CEO of the year very likely will be a robot. It remembers better than you, it counts faster than you, and it won't be angry with competitors – Jack Ma[101]

While the prospect of a CEO being completely replaced by a bunch of algorithms is somewhat distant, there are examples where this emerging technology has started to reshape how we view the definition of leadership at the top.

AI: THE DECISION MAKER

In the beginning there were PowerPoint presentations and Excel reports. And the CEO said, 'Let there be insight' and there was insight. Or rather, what followed was a gold rush of

---

[101]'CEOs could be robots in 30 years', CNBC Africa, 24 April 2017. Available from: www.cnbcafrica.com/news/2017/04/24/ceos-robots-30-years/

business analytics, business intelligence, real-time dashboards, predictive analytics, prescriptive analytics, complex event processing, and data mining tools designed to add a little more spice to the daily/weekly/monthly/quarterly reports.

Organizations are collecting more and more data every single minute of every day. It's no secret that Facebook, for example, processed 2.5 billion pieces of content and over 500 terabytes of data each day only a few years ago, pulling in 2.7 billion Likes and 300 million photos per diem.[102] Facebook also scanned a whopping 105 terabytes of data each half hour.

Of course, this is nothing new. We've been churning large volumes of data all the way back to the 1960s, when NASA took a shot at the moon. It shouldn't have been a surprise when Google gave everyone a proverbial heart attack when they revealed that they churn through almost the entire Internet every couple of days to meet our search needs.

As tools became ever more sophisticated, the amount of information available to anyone with access became unparalleled, but if you don't know what you're looking for, or don't know what questions to ask, what really is the point of holding that much information? It's a little like buying 10,000 Lego bricks of assorted shapes and sizes, tipping them on the floor and staring at them for hours thinking of all the possibilities ahead before settling on making a small house with 40 bricks. When presented with seemingly unlimited amounts of information, we default to thinking in exactly the same way as we have done many times over.

And this is where an algorithm can trump a human.

---

[102]'How big is Facebook?', 22 August 2008. Tech Crunch. Available from: https://techcrunch.com/2012/08/22/how-big-is-facebooks-data-2-5-billion-pieces-of-content-and-500-terabytes-ingested-every-day/

TIBCO CTO Matt Quinn put it well, back in 2013, when he said we should be asking ourselves:

> What's the No. 1 question that you've wanted to have answered but you were always told it was impossible? Start from there. Don't start with what data you have, start with the important question.[103]

Despite the hype, the amount of data available just got bigger, but decision-making didn't really get any better as a result. With all this ambient awareness as a by-product of having real-time dashboards and displays full of live streams of information on company or departmental performances across the organization, do we actually know what to do with this information, what is relevant, and which is actionable to help achieve the goal or task at hand? Indeed, would you even know where to look for the information or know what it looks like when you have everything within your grasp? You may not be aware of the relevance of what you possess because finding the information to put it all in context isn't clear or immediately apparent, so how can you look for it?

HOW CAN COMPANIES BE STRUCTURED AROUND A MACHINE WHO MAKES DECISIONS AT THE TOP?

We need to examine what's going wrong, what the possible solutions are, and what this means for an organization looking to embrace robotic leadership.

---

[103]Theo Priestley, 'Big Data Begs us to Ask Bigger Questions of IT', Wired, 2013. Available from: www.wired.com/insights/2013/04/big-data-begs-us-to-ask-bigger-questions-of-it/

First, humans are subject to a phenomenon known as the 'relevance paradox'. The definition of the relevance paradox explains it succinctly:[104]

> This occurs when an individual or a group of professionals are unaware of certain essential information which would guide them to make better decisions, and help them avoid inevitable, unintended consequences, and undesirable consequences. These professionals will seek only the information and advice they believe is the bare minimum amount required as opposed to what they actually need to fully meet their own or the organization's goals.

In a way, we're back to the Lego brick scenario – faced with millions of combinations and an unlimited imagination I will only build what I know, and I'll do it with the bare minimum required to achieve it so I can move on.

Another danger here for leaders and the current crop of enterprise software systems based on predictive modelling is that as the system becomes more adaptive to an individual user's needs, it learns their behaviours, filters the information according to historical data and use, and therefore potentially could deem a vital piece of information as non-critical and fail to deliver it on time.

This is especially true of atypical enterprise structures, where traditional top-down hierarchies cannot sustain the growing need for an organization to embrace a paradigm where real-time information needs to flow. Incompetence and chaos reigns.

---

[104]'Relevance Paradox', People, 2011. Available from: people.sunyit.edu/~steve/sync/idt585-fall2011/data/20110711200400/

In the early 2010s there was a growing trend of what was termed 'the social enterprise'; that is, using collaborative solutions to break down traditional hierarchical silos in the organization and open up the flow of information across the business. This led a few companies to take things a step further and break free from said organizational structures using newer (and older) methods. Wirearchy,[105] Holacracy[106] and self-organizing networks became a thing. They became popular because it was seen that as businesses evolved to move faster with the times, older structures could no longer cope to keep things moving.

Let me play with another analogy here to explain: you can't stick a Porsche engine in a VW Beetle and expect it to perform like a Porsche. Roughly translated, you can't shove a 21st-century concept in a 19th-century organization and expect it to perform either.

Another concept that reinforces this view is termed 'lateral communication'.[107]

The term lateral communication can be used interchangeably with horizontal communication. In his text entitled *Organizational Communication*, Michael J. Papa defines horizontal communication as 'the flow of messages across functional areas at a given level of an organization'. People at the same level 'communicate directly without going through several levels of organization'. Given this elasticity, members within an organization have an easier time with 'problem-solving, information sharing across different

---

[105]'What is Wirearchy?', Wirearchy. Available from: wirearchy.com/what-is-wirearchy/
[106]Holacracy. Available from: www.holacracy.org/
[107]'Lateral Communication', Wikipedia. Available from: en.wikipedia.org/wiki/Lateral_communication

work groups, and task coordination between departments or project teams'. The use of lateral or horizontal communication in the workplace 'can also enhance morale and afford a means for resolving conflicts'.

The problem with hierarchy is that it enforces unnecessary rigidity with the overall control and flow of information it aims to bestow. It rarely takes into account a hidden network of experts that exists outside of these boundaries in an enterprise, which needs to be tapped into.

> Networking has always been an essential social skill founded on the interdependence of people. We all rely on the support and cooperation of others to achieve our goals. Networking within the enterprise involves bonding, sharing expertise and investing time and effort into others. It's a natural operating model which has remained untapped for years because we always seek comfort in building walls between resources in order to correctly label them.[108]

Networking is recognized as a major influence on an employee's ability to work well in an organization and be successful. In fact, the most successful people in the world possess the capability to influence and shape the opinions of others, which today places greater emphasis on the types of networking a person does.

Internal enterprise networks have a major impact on organizational effectiveness, but more importantly, these types of networks provide major business advantages for the participants.

[108]Michelle Wierzgac, 'Here's how to engage the power of your informal network', AZ Big Media, 24 August 2019. Available from: https://azbigmedia.com/business/jobs/heres-how-to-engage-the-power-of-your-informal-networks/

There are major advantages when comparing a hierarchy against a networked enterprise community: for example, formal and hierarchical divisional entities consist of areas such as Operations, Performance Management, Human Resources, Sales, Manufacturing... They are defined by organizational boundaries so are rigid and hard to change. Within them exist work domains such as virtual or project-led teams who are organized and task-oriented; they cross organizational boundaries but tend to have a 'closed membership'.

A networked organizational community, however, is shaped informally, with interests, is self-motivated, is more innovative due to lack of constraints, has a network of experts and knowledge communities, exists outside organizational boundaries and works on an 'open membership'.

The most effective enterprise networks contain high-functioning people who are extremely skilled, knowledgeable, powerful, and who have strong personal networks. The informal network without the hierarchy and bureaucracy encourages the most interaction and achieves the most positive results.

Support for organizational structures like this is important and noteworthy because they offer a glimpse into the benefits of an enterprise driven by AI leadership. A robot CEO suffers no managerial ego or need to withhold information and data that could be utilized by a workforce. A robot CEO would also be able to drive and fuel a network of experts and communities exposed by methods discussed above through:

- Timely identification of subject matter experts (SMEs) and stakeholders. Avoids duplication of effort by finding individuals in an enterprise with experience in the topic or relevant parties to involve. Like a tag cloud in a blog, topics of interest are associated with the real SMEs for rapid location of knowledge;

- Facilitating reorganizations to understand how the business networks interact and translate them into the formal organizational charts;
- Identification of the impact of a key person leaving, both internally and externally;
- Allowing new employees to integrate more quickly into a company by seeking expertise and building relationships and their own networks;
- Understanding customer interactions and how better to serve them;
- Identification of the key influencers within a group.

What we need to do now is start to re-examine, in this new light, the organizational research that has gone before and the impetus that could be heralded in by an AI boardroom. Collaborative software efforts and loose org structures have been tried before, but without an integral ingredient: an AI leader.

There are two rather interesting examples from different industries that highlight both the good and the bad in this situation, then we'll go on to see just how being led by an AI management team would differ.

VALVE CORPORATION

In 1999, Valve Corporation – the game developer behind the hugely successful *Half-Life* and *Portal* games – spoke to

Gamasutra[109] to shed light on their design process. It was a fascinating insight into how the company structured itself around teams, or what they called 'Cabals'.

> The first few months of the Cabal process were somewhat nerve-wracking for those outside the process. It wasn't clear that egos could be suppressed enough to get anything done, or that a vision of the game filtered through a large number of people would be anything other than bland. As it turned out, the opposite was true; the people involved were tired of working in isolation and were energized by the collaborative process, and the resulting designs had a consistent level of polish and depth that hadn't been seen before.
>
> Internally, once the success of the Cabal process was obvious, mini-Cabals were formed to come up with answers to a variety of design problems. These mini-Cabals would typically include people most affected by the decision, as well as try to include people completely outside the problem being addressed in order to keep a fresh perspective on things. We also kept membership in the initial Cabal somewhat flexible and we quickly started to rotate people through the process every month or so, always including a few people from the last time, and always making sure we had a cross section of the company. This helped to prevent burnout, and ensured that everyone involved in the process had experience using the results of Cabal decisions.

[109]Ken Birdwell, 'The Cabal: Valve's Design Process for Creating *Half-Life*', Gamasutra, 10 December 1999. Available from: www.gamasutra.com/view/feature/3408/ the_cabal_valves_design_process_.php?page=1

What was interesting was that when they created the Cabal process they threw out job descriptions because they found them too constraining (and couldn't hire externally the people they required because of them).

> Instead, we would create our own ideal by combining the strengths of a cross section of the company, putting them together in a group we called the 'Cabal'.

I decided to get in touch with Gabe Newell, the CEO of Valve, to understand more about his own opinions on hierarchy versus network organizational models.

> 'The simple answer is that hierarchy is good for repeatability and measurability, whereas self-organizing networks are better at invention,' Gabe said. 'There are a lot of side effects and consequences. The lack of titles (roles) is primarily an internal signalling tool.
>
> 'The alternate answer is that organizations that think they are hierarchical actually don't gain advantage by it (they actually have hidden networks), and that the hierarchical appearance is the result of rent-seeking.'

HOW DOES LEADERSHIP STYLE CHANGE IN THE FACE OF INTELLIGENT AUTOMATION?

What are the opportunities in front of us if we embrace intelligent automation and robotic decision makers?

Bridgewater Associates, who manage the world's largest hedge fund to the tune of $160 billion, have already begun work to automate most of the firm's senior management through algorithms. The founder, billionaire Ray Dalio, wanted to ensure that the firm continued to operate according to his guiding principles and vision even when he's no longer around.

Deep Knowledge Ventures (DKV), a Hong-Kong-based venture capital firm, appointed an artificial intelligence to its board of directors in 2014. By 2017, 'VITAL' (Validating Investment Tool for Advancing Life) was credited with bringing the company back from the brink and work had already begun on VITAL 2.0.

ONE AI TO RULE THEM ALL AND IN
THE DARKNESS BLIND THEM

There's a misconception that there will be one God-like AI ruling everything, and this isn't true. We already have several examples of AI evolving, such as Amazon Alexa, Siri, Google Assistant, never mind the thousands of start-ups creating chatbots for us to engage with. There will be many more AI examples that unfold over time, and who knows, a handful of superintelligences, but there will never be a Skynet overlord.

Why should we fear a world filled with different types of AI when we share a world with different types of humans? – and are we duty-bound to treat it ethically, morally, with the same rights we give ourselves?

According to the Bible, if God created Man in his own image, what image will a true AI take if it creates itself? And under no illusion, I firmly believe that AI begets AI and we'll see true emergence out of itself, not born from human hands at a keyboard.

And as a result, what could we learn about our own humanity from something that is artificial?

If AI frees us to pursue that quest, to push the boundaries of what humans can achieve, to travel further into the universe, peer into the quantum realm, cure disease, then is appointing a robot to lead a company or humanity into a new era such a bad idea after all, if they can take care of all the things that prevent us from these goals?

So, choose your new overlord.

Should we be slaves to the definition of what it means to be human today, or do we take a leap of faith and embrace what it could mean for us tomorrow?

14

Everything is Connected

by Kate O'Neill, futurist, founder of KO Insights, author and speaker

Everything is connected. And not just in a figurative sense. The Internet of things and people means that, increasingly, both humans and objects are constantly connected to the invisible yet omnipresent Internet. The question is: do we really need 'chips with everything'? How much is too much when connecting every available resource to the Internet, and who really benefits from all the data and connections we are making and solidifying? Surveillance capitalism is becoming unstoppable, so why do we need an AI-driven toothbrush that tells our dentist and healthcare insurer we didn't brush twice on Tuesday? In this chapter we look at the slices of life that are best served without a side of chips.

The future isn't what we think.

It isn't inevitable that it will slip towards dystopia, and it isn't merely some vast unknowable thing. The future is as simple as this next moment coming up, and then the one after that. The future is moments from now, hours from now, tomorrow, and next Tuesday. It's as much the moments you can see ahead of you that influence you as the ones you can't easily foresee and can't imagine shaping.

And it's not what we think. It's what we do.

That's how it all connects. The future is what we do, what we did, what we decided, what others decided for us. The future connects to the past. The past connects to the present. Everything touches and influences everything else. In the same way you decide not to spend all of your money today so that you won't be entirely broke next Monday, we have the chance to choose what we do that will leave the world with more options and more resources in whatever time horizon we are looking towards.

FASTER, MORE COMPLEX, MORE CONNECTED, MORE DYSTOPIAN?

If you've ever thought that life seems to be going faster and getting more complicated, that's not just your imagination: technology has been speeding up the manufacture and production of goods for quite some time, and newer technologies keep accelerating how we communicate, how we consume, and how we experience everything else around us. Meanwhile, the introduction of these technologies has added more complexity to the world and to our lives.

The good news and bad news is that with all that complexity and acceleration, everything also becomes more connected. And this exponential connectedness brings *scale*. Things matter at scale and in aggregate that may not matter as much individually, and it's up to us to learn to recognize these systems, to insist on better from companies, from governments, and from ourselves.

It's hard to insist on better when we don't have a shared vision of the future we want, yet the default mode of talking about the future across most cultures often lacks nuance. Just about all we have is reduced to a dichotomy: dystopia versus utopia. And since most of us can agree that utopia won't be happening, we're left to conceive of and plan for the future through a lens of dystopian vocabulary.

This dichotomy of dystopia versus utopia is more than useless: it's dangerous. The falseness of that dichotomy and the despair of being left to accept dystopia keeps us from focusing on and addressing what we can each do every day to actively create a better future. We need to leave dystopia behind and invent a new framework and new language.

Our new mindset should involve a more holistic, integrative, both/and kind of thinking because we need to be able to talk about what's happening that's both constructive and destructive, and we need to be able to do so on both the human scale and the humanity scale. We need to consider both individual, human-level consequences of decisions and broader, more integrated consequences on communities, society at large, humanity at scale.

HUMAN DATA AT SCALE

We live in a world that is more enmeshed by data than ever, and more economically interdependent than ever, partly as a result of that data mesh. The global economy could only become as interconnected as it has with the Internet and with the digital transformation of supply chains, providing greater transparency and trackability for goods and services around the world.

Meanwhile, let's be clear: the conversation about 'digital transformation' is really a conversation about data connectedness. And the vast majority of that data is somehow measuring or collected around human experience. It's the things that we do, the things that we say, the connections that we have, the relationships that we have, everywhere we go – it all gets collected, aggregated and used by business, governments and other entities to *determine* our human experiences.

Even the decisions we make about what data to share have repercussions on the data that shapes our identity, and the avatars of people assumed to be like us. Privacy has typically been thought about from a personal, individual sense but, perhaps even more critically, because of predictive inferences[110] that can be made with big data analytics and AI from even incomplete data, your behaviour shapes models that can also be used to model and predict other people's behaviour.

As systems increasingly come online that can integrate data sets from disparate places, we can fundamentally never fully know what is known about us. Our collective data can be accessed, collected, modelled, predicted, and further built into interactions in ways that can 'nudge' us through addiction algorithms to co-operate and sometimes unwittingly play into a larger scheme of data collection.

---

[110]Sandra Wachter and Brent Mittelstadt, 'A Right to Reasonable Inferences: Re-Thinking Data Protection Law in the Age of Big Data and AI', *Columbia Business Law Review*, 2019(1), Oxford Internet Institute, University of Oxford. Available from: papers.ssrn.com/sol3/papers.cfm?abstract_id=3248829

When we look at it that certain way, data shows us just how connected we are – with each other and with our past and future selves. You're connected to your own destiny, to your own past actions, and to your own future in ways that were never as fixed before. Moreover, our everyday human experiences increasingly generate data and, in tandem, our everyday human experiences are increasingly determined by data and optimized by algorithms. The trails of data we leave behind us become a feedback loop of our future opportunities and our digital and physical surroundings that conform to our stated and unstated preferences and world views.

Look at the 'filter bubble' that gets created partly by what Google, Facebook, Twitter, etc. want us to see, and partly by our media choices. Look at bias in hiring algorithms: Amazon had an automated recruiting tool that penalized résumés with the word 'women's'.[111] Humans don't make hiring decisions without bias, so we can do better, but with machines we're handing over the keys. Look at predictive policing[112] and law enforcement algorithms: as a 2019 *Guardian* article puts it, 'One officer told the researchers that "young black men are more likely to be stopped and searched than young white men, and that's purely down to human bias. That human bias is then introduced into the data sets, and bias is then generated in the outcomes of the application of those data sets".'

---

[111]Jeffery Dastin, 'Amazon scraps secret AI recruiting tool that showed bias against women', 11 October 2018, Reuters, Available from: https://www.reuters.com/article/ us-amazon-com-jobs-automation-insight-idUSKCN1MK08G

[112]Jamie Grierson, 'Predictive policing poses discrimination risk', *Guardian*, 16 September 2019. Available from: www.theguardian.com/uk-news/2019/sep/16/ predictive-policing-poses-discrimination-risk-thinktank-warns

Machines are what we encode of ourselves, yet rather than encoding the best of ourselves, too often we are carelessly building automated echo chambers and indulging in self-fulfilling prophecies.

FOCUSING ON WHAT MATTERS: TECH HUMANISM, NOT TECHNO-SOLUTIONISM

With all this said, it's easy to see emerging technology as a problem humanity faces, partly because human experiences will increasingly be shaped by algorithms, scaled by automation, and amplified through machine learning. But the problems with technology are rarely about technology; instead, they tend to reveal the decisions of the humans who built everything and set the rules.

These same technologies, given better input, offer tremendous opportunities to facilitate solving human problems at scale more efficiently than ever, while offering better human connectedness. This is not techno-solutionism: rather than leading with technology as our salvation, and without placing too much trust in big tech companies or big tech platforms, we can and must look to the sheer *capacity* of technology as a strategic asset in solving human problems – and humanity's problems – at scale. But to keep our results focused on better human outcomes, our approach must begin with and remain grounded in humanity and human values, understanding what humanity is, what it means to be human, and so on, and then must use technology to amplify those characteristics. It must be global digital transformation that keeps humans at the centre: with an emphasis on meaningful human experiences, guided by strategic purpose.

After all, the central thesis of my work is that one of the distinct and driving characteristics of what makes humans human is that *humans crave meaning*. And meaning at every level – whether in terms of semantics, relevance, significance, patterns, cosmic or existential – is always about *what matters*. Even the meaning in a business context, which is purpose, can be seen as *intention around what matters*. Innovation becomes *what is going to matter*. If we will let ourselves see everything through a connected framework of meaning, we will tend to focus on what matters.

WATCH OUT FOR ABSURDITY

Even amid the meaningful events of human life, we encounter absurd moments. It's not that absurdity is the inverse of meaning, per se. It exists in a kind of tension with meaning. That tension can be enlightening, such as in surrealist art: 'Ceci n'est pas une pipe'. But for the purposes of experience design, the general principle is: where meaning is well defined, absurdity is scarce, and where there is absurdity, meaning struggles to exist.

It's the absurd human experiences created by technology that threaten to overtake our world. Absurd in the sense that we don't know whether to say please and thank you to our voice assistants. It's absurd every time we have to check an 'I'm not a robot' box to 'confirm' our humanity to a machine. It's absurd being in an Amazon Go grocery store and not being able to take products off the shelves for other shoppers who need our help because of the risk of being charged for their products. It's a 'this is not a pipe' version of reality without the enlightenment. Scale raises the stakes on the design of interactions and shines a spotlight on anywhere

166

we forgot to build in a sense of meaning and what matters. That's an easy problem to have, because 'what matters' at first may seem straightforward and may change dramatically with scale. Because experience at scale changes culture. Because experience at scale *is* culture.

We don't want to let absurd interactions and experiences scale into an absurd culture. In the near term, absurdity is a far greater risk than full-blown dystopia. This is part of the language we're missing to discuss the future. We talk about the freedom of automation replacing meaningless and trivial tasks, but as more and more of our human experiences are automated, if we want to avoid scaling absurdity, we will want these experiences to be infused with a human sense of meaning.

WE'RE ALL INDIVIDUALS, AND WE'RE NOT

With decisions at scale, individuality becomes a dot in a pointillist painting. The whole of the picture shapes culture. That's not to say the dot doesn't matter; of course it does on its own scale. That's also not to say that individuality, identity and personal autonomy are not important constructs; of course they are, not least because out of individual identity comes a consciousness that seeks meaning and everything associated with it: purpose, significance, etc. But one dot's individual 'dotness' doesn't override the importance of the rest of the dots. Both individual rights *and* collective human rights matter. We need to plan for the future on the dot and painting levels simultaneously: at human scale and humanity scale.

In the social justice space, there is a commonly cited notion: 'impact matters more than intent'. In other words, your good intentions mean little if you perform them in a way that ignores their outcome and the harms they may do to others. That's because the moment you take an action, it very likely affects other people.

As I write this, the world is facing a pandemic, and the primary mechanism for containing its spread is for everyone to recognize our role in an interconnected network of contagion. Contagion that could reach, infect and even kill someone we care about. But mostly it will devastate people we don't know personally, and that should matter, too – though it can be hard to care about that which seems removed and disconnected from us.

Perhaps we need better reminders of how connected we truly are. After all, the entire *universe* is interconnected. Whenever you need a reminder to think about yourself in a more cosmically connected way, remember that the carbon, nitrogen, iron and other elements in our bodies were all part of long-ago dying stars, perhaps far beyond our own galaxy. In ways literal enough to metaphorically blow your mind, we are in the universe, and the universe is within us.

We think we are shaped by external forces, but we have more influence on the 'external' world than we think. We tend to think of ourselves as small, independent figures, and what difference could our decisions possibly make? This demonstrates that perhaps we need a new way to think about our decisions.

HOW DO WE GO FORWARD?

We tend to spend a lot of time thinking about what could go wrong and less time on what could go right. In my experience, a pretty good amount of what goes wrong happens as a result of not having thought enough about what could go right. Because 'going right' for many experiences means achieving scale, and scale is a stress test for how meaningful experiences are, and how much thought has gone into their impact.

But there's a power in the kind of integrative thinking that allows us to see both/and: we can integrate all of our thinking, acknowledge all the possibilities of what's going on around us, acknowledge the reality of what's happening, acknowledge the full range of possible outcomes out of any given thing that happens to us. But then choose the direction of our action.

I have always loved the Emily Dickinson quote: 'Hope inspires the good to reveal itself'. The way I apply that in my life and work is to think of hope as a tool of *focus and refocus*. Whenever things change, whenever anything happens around us, we have the opportunity to choose where we'll put our energy, our focus, our time and our attention. But whatever we feel hope for, we are also compelling ourselves to work for. Optimism obligates us. Optimism isn't about seeing only the good: it's about committing to the good we see. Wherever we can see a better future, we have a responsibility to work towards it.

With data and algorithmic optimization, we go forward by fully acknowledging that algorithmic experiences can go very, very wrong. And that in very real ways, our own lives are connected to those outcomes. Having made that acknowledgement, we must then decide to address it, to unpack it, to improve it. Where we collect data for opportunity, we must use it to create more meaningful experiences and better outcomes. It is up to us to shape the future in the way our hopes are asking us to work for.

A WHOLE NEW VIEW

Within the last decade, I have begun to characterize my career as 'helping humanity prepare for an increasingly tech-driven future'. But the future of human experience is deeply integrated – everything depends on everything else. Our fates are interlinked. So humanity has to prepare for the tech-driven future at scale by preparing for and mitigating everything else at scale: climate catastrophe, the cyclical expansion and collapse of globalization; ongoing geopolitical conflict; financial market upheaval; the legacy of racism, slavery and colonialism; algorithmically enhanced culture wars; the decline of trust; extreme wealth inequity and widespread poverty, etc.

We also need to prepare in a way that respects the human scale of life, experiences, well-being and rights – all without jeopardizing the natural ecosystem, non-human animals, or the potential for future life to flourish.

Given all this, is regulation the only thing that can save us from the absurdity at scale that disconnects us from a better and more meaningful future? We will probably have an ongoing need for increased and smarter regulation, but can we also do something more proactive? Can we advance an entirely new world view?

This view would have to shake off the cynicism of dystopian defaults and instead use integrative thinking and strategic optimism to develop a unifying framework for what an inclusive, connected better future for all looks like; create new curricula that include early education on AI and the implications of algorithmic bias; identify new measures and standards of success, and more.

This approach would need to build around exponential change in multiple areas, like artificial intelligence, workplace automation, climate change, and more. It can work alongside existing unifying frameworks for improvement of life on a global scale, like the Sustainable Development Goals from the United Nations. These 17 goals interconnect in important ways: ending poverty in all its forms everywhere (SDG #1) and ensuring inclusive and equitable quality education for all (SDG #4) are listed as separate goals, but they're likely to be related both in approach and in results.

While we work collectively on this new view and broader framework, we can start by adding a new decision checklist to our workflow when we introduce new experiences, new products, new interactions, new modalities of communication, etc.

1 To ground our decisions in a meaning-oriented view of human experience, we must ask 'What *matters*?'
2 To focus our innovative efforts on the meaningful future for humanity, we must ask, 'What is *going to matter*?'
3 We need to consider these questions at *both* the human, individual scale *and* at the scale of society and humanity.
4 We must consider the *impact* they may have.
5 And we must consider these questions across a wide range of areas such as the SDGs, across systems, with explicit acknowledgement of the interconnectedness of all things. Systems thinking – putting something into the context of a larger whole – may not save us but reductive thinking will almost certainly ruin us.

We *must* make decisions so that they will make the best futures. This is not about slowing down innovation (although sometimes a little slowness can be a gift); it's meant to make our contributions more thoughtful, more aligned, and more meaningful. It's meant to help us innovate what is going to matter.

It's the best way to the brightest future for us all.

15

Longevity is not the Game Changer, Retirement Is

by Anne Skare Nielsen, Chief Futurist at Universal Futurist

Human lifespans are increasing all over the world. And this poses various pressing questions: how can we fund ageing populations and longer retirements? How do we mitigate intergenerational conflicts? And how will we spend these longer, healthier lives? This chapter explores the shift from retirement to 'pretirement' to prepare businesses and individuals for less linear, more meaningful life plans.

YOU WILL WORK UNTIL YOU DIE. HERE'S
HOW TO MAKE THE BEST OF IT!

In 1947 life expectancy was 85.

In 2007 it was 103.

Children born in 2020 have an estimated life expectancy between 80 and 120 years, depending on where you live.[113]

[113] 'We'll Live to 100 – How Can We Afford It?', World Economic Forum, May 2017. Available from: www3.weforum.org/docs/WEF_White_Paper_We_Will_Live_to_100.pdf

If you are younger than 50, dear reader, there is very little chance that you are going to retire in your sixties. Retirement is likely to soon become a phenomenon of the past. Or a privilege of the very wealthy.

But don't be sad. Retirement is not that healthy for you, and it's not a given.

Imagine this: You have saved up to retire after a long, relatively satisfying working life. The young bank advisor looks at your numbers, smiles, and then states without much empathy: *'Yes, it looks pretty good. With your current consumption pattern, you can maintain your standard of living until you reach the age of 71. If you plan on living longer, you need to downgrade, or – you can choose our new "Going out in style package", where we will send you a little pill on your 71st birthday so you can kick the bucket the day after.'*

Absurd scenario? Yes. But the alternative is just as ridiculous: entering a future where many, many, many senior citizens will leave the labour market and go on mental and creative screensaver for 10-20-30, even 40 years!

'Living a long life' has always been a success criterion for welfare societies.

But it has come as a surprise that a *long* life is not the same as a *good* life.

Challenge number 1: We need to talk about ageing and becoming a senior as a good thing. After all, it's a destination many of us will reach, no matter what we do (and it's certainly preferable to the alternative).

Unfortunately, we don't see old age that way. Instead of being a level up in prosperity and creativity or investments in humanity, retirement is at best 'our final vacation'. The last resting place before death.

Are you just going to accept that?

All over the world, public expenditure is in the process of being absorbed by medical health insurance and retirement for the elderly. The ageing society is a 'hard trend' – a condition – around the globe.

And yes, it creates a massive market for care, self-help products, and even robotic baby seals, but time is also more than ripe for radical change.

For many – and not just the young – the concept of retirement has become hopelessly limiting. It is a relic of the past, an industrial invention initially meant to be a small 'token of appreciation' to a limited group of people or a buffer-tool to pull workers in and out of the labour market.

There is nothing 'natural' about retirement. The version we see as 'normal' today was created just 100 years ago – we are only in the third generation of modern retirement.

'THE SILVER TSUNAMI' WILL CHANGE THE RULES OF THE GAME: FROM *RETIREMENT* TO *PRETIREMENT*

As the world moves towards a new paradigm of productivity, 'old' should not mean 'obsolete'. Time and muscle strength are not as essential as brainpower, wisdom and a willingness to learn and adapt.

Radical game changers call for radical reforms: what the future would like us to do is to transform the *retirement* system into a *pretirement* system.

Instead of 'postponing the inevitable', we should turn the unpleasant notion of ageing into the most potent fertilizer of the future: work until you die but take breaks throughout your entire life.

Breaks to learn new things.

Time-outs to be with those we love.

Carve out a piece of our lives to be a force in the local community.

A breather to collect new insights into what lies ahead and not just treading water at work or spinning the hamster wheel.

And yes, we will work until we die – if we are willing and able.

Does that scare you? Because it shouldn't – there is something much worse than working till you die.

RETIREMENT CREATED OLD AGE – NOT THE OTHER WAY AROUND

What wears you down is not old age.

Well, yes, if you are a Polish coal miner, you will be exhausted at 60. And a Norwegian butcher can also be tired and worn down. Just as a Spanish biologist can fall from a tree, a Chinese lifeguard can develop anxiety, and a Turkish lecturer can lose his voice. And totally fair if, as a retired medical secretary, you never want to answer a phone ever again and prefer to replace people's warts with roses of the garden.

But for many, many people, old age does not mean the batteries have lost the ability to recharge. On the contrary, the idea of remaining in the labour market can be the best-case scenario – but of course, under different, freer, and more value-creating conditions.

Consider also that in the future, the elderly will not be afraid that there is 'not enough' (like their grandparents) or 'not to have lived' (like their parents) – they will be frightened 'not to have made a difference'. That all the hours, all the wear and tear, all the meetings and planning won't be seen or felt anywhere. That you were never really here.

A senior citizen rebellion is just around the corner – expect a revolution that can make the final phase in life the most exciting one of all.

Let's start with a fact: it's not because you're getting old that you're retiring – it's the other way around. You're retiring. And then you get 'old'.

What is 'natural' for humans is to be in vigour. Being a valuable part of a community has always been a must. So yes, we will grow old – but that 'old' has to define what you can or cannot do is a story we invented ourselves.

It goes something like this:

- Retirement created old age as we know it today.
- The industrial age created abundance.
- And thus room for some to be made redundant.
- The industrial age made room for an organized retirement system. And it was well suited for the challenges of that era.

But times are changing.

AMONG CAVEMEN, THERE WERE NO RETIREES

Throughout human history, it has never been 'normal' to stop working abruptly. If you were alive, then you did something. And if you stopped doing something, it was because you were dead or incapacitated.

The weary, sick or worn out were slowly phased out of physical work, transitioning to sedentary needlework, storytelling, or – if wise – training the next generations.

The fear of 'the slow death' was real.

If you were not wealthy, it was advantageous to have many children, hoping that one of them (often one of the daughters) could take care of you. The only alternatives were 'the crappy model': die slow, lonely and painful – or the 'dignified model': as in Greenland, where the elderly went back to 'mother' – meaning a one-way trip out on the ice or into the sea.

In the many thousands of years before the welfare society emerged, it took some resilience to be alive. Today we falsely believe that 'a long life' – that you can live until you turn 100 – is a new thing. But it is not. If you could get through the first 15–20 years of your life without getting sick, having a rock dropped on your head, or getting into a fight, a war, or an accident, then the probability of living for a long time was very high – i.e. 80–90 years.

Men have furnished our social structures so that authority and power naturally came to them with age. But on the other hand, old women have often been disregarded as being 'past their prime'. To this day, we acknowledge men who get children at a late age as virile and courageous, while women who give birth very late in life are a bit icky, reckless or egocentric.

The human race is an extremely resilient species. We can handle temperature fluctuations from -50 to +50°C, train to breathe underwater for several minutes, and live in the thin layers of air. We can even survive on fast food, cheap doughnuts and mouldy cheese. Where a gazelle just gives up when caught, humans keep fighting.

In Nordic mythology, Thor, the god of thunder, wrestles with Aelde (old Nordic for old age) and is brought to his knees but does not lose the battle. We cherish these stories to remind ourselves of not giving up. And we need to tap back into that feisty spirit.

RETIREMENT WAS ONCE A REALLY, REALLY GOOD IDEA

The ageing community is a huge challenge today – a condition we see coming, but which we have not yet really grasped. One of the main concerns is that our welfare societies are collapsing, polarized by the rich and healthy on the one hand, and the sick and poor on the other. This disparity is nothing new, but after decades we've still failed to find a solution. What is new is that we now feel committed to ensuring a certain quality of life for the elderly – and this will be expensive.

From the Middle Ages to the rise of the welfare society, the lonely old people tumbled through the streets. Sick, alone, and huddled. They had to beg and steal to survive. Socially oriented politicians established workhouses and Homes of the Poor, where residents lay in layers, carved stones, and ate porridge. People's expectations of life were low – which is the easiest way to deliver quality: to meet low expectations.

The problem we face today is not that we live longer. It is that the expectations of what life should be when you get old are very, very high. And it is rightly being called a bomb under the welfare system:

- We already have elderly citizens galore;
- They are retiring fast, thus leaving the productivity circus;
- They have high expectations of life, both for themselves and for others.

179

You don't have to be a futurist to see we will hit a wall in a speeding vehicle. Postponing the retirement age makes the road slightly longer, yet we are still going to hit the wall.

Can we come up with something smarter and better?

Yes, we can. We have to craft contemporary solutions that fit the time we live in instead of copying the past.

If you are like most people, then a part of you believes that the older you get, the more relaxed, calm and cosy life should be. You shouldn't work as much, and your life might have been challenging or boring, so your last years are there to be enjoyed, yes?

But know this: this version of 'old age' has been formulated by politicians and the modern healthcare system. If we understand 'old age' as the phase of life where you have to withdraw from society and enjoy a well-deserved staycation with a crossword puzzle and a blanket over your legs, propaganda from the top has made it so. Somebody wanted you to accept that retirement is something you deserve!

Why is the retirement age set around 65? Are there biologically oriented analyses underlying this figure? Was it on Moses' tablets when he came down from the mountain? Is it inscribed in our DNA? No. The retirement age is 65 because, in 1887, Bismarck thought it was a good number. Bismarck needed a solution that could curb the progress of the Marxists, and he could introduce it without much cost because penicillin had not yet been invented. Under the unhealthy urban conditions of the time, few survived that long. So retirement as a 65-year-old sounded great.

As the factories and cities took over agricultural work in economic terms, the new leaders were very sceptical about whether older people could adapt to the new way of working. There was a pronounced aversion towards the old in the modern dynamic industrial society. And out of this aversion, a whole school of health and social ideologies was born, seeking to find evidence that when you were over 60, you were inept, useless, and had lost all 'mental elasticity'. And if you search, then you shall find, as we know.

If only old people could understand that they had to go home and bake cookies or smoke cigars, everything would be so much easier, faster, and wonderfully industrial, the new elite agreed. But an ageing workforce said no. Humankind is not suitable for unemployment. And hey, we just made that colossal transformation from agricultural to industrial labour. Work is no longer something we do at home, it's a place we go to.

It took many years to educate, retrain and convince the workforce to believe that with age, declining productivity follows. As a curiosity, no such thing existed for slaves in the 19th-century US. Slaves could work long and hard no matter the amount of grey hair, as long as they were healthy and uninjured. Why? Because there was a capitalist interest in exploiting the labour of a slave for as long as possible. We should always be careful when we label people 'good for business'. Historically, seniors had to enter or leave the labour market when it suited business. And if not by free will, then brainwashing had to ensure it.

And that's the real problem: people began to believe it – that being old is equivalent to being weak and slow. And when many believe it, it becomes a self-fulfilling prophecy. If we treat older people as frail, it is significantly easier for them to see themselves as feeble and fragile.

Interestingly enough, it is the unions, politicians and specific member organizations that make the most out of portraying older people as weak. While we, as ordinary people, admire the 70-year-old marathon runner who overpowers her peers or the kite surfer of 92 who died on the beach surrounded by his much younger friends here in Copenhagen, where I live, the truth is that older people are as diverse as everyone else. You do not suddenly get a whole lot in common with the others at 65 just because you are 65. You can be worn down when you are 22. And you can be a mountain climber at 78.

Helping citizens invest in their own long lives and preventing suffering is a societal mission. We should invest heavily in this from the time we are born. This requires a reward system to get people to stay healthy and communities that support them because few have the discipline to resist temptation or pull themselves out of life's misery holes.

Times are changing. They always have. And of course, the economy and the institutions must follow. First and foremost: stop putting people in boxes created by statistics and prejudice and instead let the individual take centre stage.

OLD AGE, SHAKE YOUR PANTS: WE WILL BREAK YOU!

The obvious fix would be to retire many times throughout your life. Instead of aiming at one big break at the end of life, you can spread out your breaks throughout your life. You have to save up for that yourself, but not without support from your colleagues and an innovative pretirement plan. This plan will help you anticipate life's ups and downs. Take a break when you have young children before a life crisis hits, or well before your job gets automated. Throughout your life, you will have periods of high work intensity, and in others, you'll have time to read, sleep, play, educate yourself, and exercise. You'll be a human being, not just a human doing.

Who then takes care of my work while I'm away, you say?

Well, either the job is gone, taken over by a robot, or you have grown tired of it, or your colleagues are doing it – but your 'job' when pretired is to come back, full of energy and with a new skill set. The premise, of course, is that a permanent job in your industry, at the factory or office, no longer exists and that we are all 'sentenced to freedom'. Whether we are butchers, teachers, doctors or truck drivers, job security will instead come from your skills: your ability to learn new things, work well with others and create a kind of value that can be felt and experienced.

It will not be measured in how many hours you can press a button on a keyboard or a machine, or how large a dose of boring PowerPoint presentations you can endure.

I can easily imagine that our children, when the labour market has become theirs, will have a working week where they perform at their peak 2–4 days a week, some days 2 hours, other days 14 hours, and when they think of their parents – who, like robots, drove off at the same time and came home at the same time – they will laugh and talk about how inefficient work was in the good old days.

A radically changed future requires radically changed behaviour – today. This requires an overhauled attitude to old age, to working life, to value creation and productivity. Then we can create a labour market that we not only 'can endure' but that we can love in good times and bad.

Many trends will push us in this direction:

- The boomers are retiring. Did they finish their youthful rebellion, or will they start a new one? Many of them have money, power and strong opinions. And they need to take a new position in society if they want to be heard and taken seriously;

- Tired, tired, tired. The workforce is tired of stupid systems, leaders with no vision, and management that only focuses on growth and money;
- Others are doing it. In the world of sports, we have recognized that restitution is as essential as the training itself. Why should work be any different?
- Science is pointing it out. Time and productivity are not related simplistically. As an example, studies show that if you are older than 42, you should only work 3–4 days a week if you have an office job. At this age you are competent, you are fast running out of fucks to give, and it's much better for your mood to go all-in in shorter time spans. Spreading the same work over more days will only make you cranky and irritable;
- The sharing economy. We are entering a future of new, dedicated communities that could revolve around setting each other free. No need to own everything when we can share more things, and live just as well or better. A definition of being rich is to 'have access to' the things you need to live a happy life;
- Your belongings will be able to generate an income for you – for example, by producing and bartering energy through your house or car. Many expenses can become assets: houses, cars, clothes, prams, etc;
- Final destination: Nursing home – or running for the hills? You don't have to if you don't want to. Maybe you will reside with your friends or grandkids. There will be more private and semi-public opportunities – from hotel-like luxury amenities to more accessible, inexpensive hippy retreats or dorms.

The greatest fear – what we have feared the most since the beginning of time – is not growing old. Nor is it being unemployed. It is that no one needs us.

The most important task we have right now might be this: to create a society where we need each other from the cradle to the grave – regardless of background, age or income level.

And it can be done. If we want to and ask for the necessary changes. Together.

After all, we certainly have come a long way since our first human ancestors arrived on planet Earth:

1905: The health service wants to get rid of old people.
William Osler, the co-founder of Johns Hopkins Hospital (one of the giants of American medicine), states that all men over 60 should retire because, by that time, they have lost all 'mental elasticity'.

1906: Economic management and productivity theory drives
you out to the sidelines.
Economists in the UK and US state that the highest productivity will be achieved if you start working as a 15-year-old and end as a 65-year-old. The bureaucratic bus is on the move.

1920: Youthful hedonism is the way forward. Old is boring.
The Roaring Twenties. The youth culture roars. Parties, enjoyment and consumerism take hold.

Consumption, and especially overconsumption, has up until now been frowned upon. After all, we are poor and must always fight for what we have. Illness and consumption are related to each other. In earlier days, you could be arrested on the street for flashing an expensive, imported silk scarf.

But the new progress is slowly making consumption a huge plus. Those who consume are alive. Those who live above capacity live well, and signal that they are willing to spend their time in the big societal machine. You have to consume and create – if not, you will be consumed yourself.

Where frugality has been a virtue before, wastefulness begins to signal belief in one's own abilities and freedom from eternal concerns, which have otherwise always been a dominant part of life.

1929: Depression – Can you follow us as we step on the accelerator?
Depression strikes in Europe and the US. The banking crisis and industrial meltdown. Your savings are gone. Fifty million Americans are poor and unemployed. The hopelessness spreads. The jobs that exist are only for young people. You join a union, even if it is dangerous.

1933: New Deal. You get the first state pension or annuity.
Roosevelt is carrying out significant reforms that support the disabled and families with many children, and rejoice! – the first real pension sees the light of day. Like Bismarck, Roosevelt set the retirement age at 65, but since the majority died at 63, he moved it to 62. A state-funded retirement, funded by your pay cheque, is now the norm.

1934: Hang on to the assembly line.
The seniors refuse to leave the labour market and retire. To 'break them', the factory owners are turning up the speed of the assembly lines. Eleanor Roosevelt runs campaigns designed to convince workers of the joy of retiring from the job market and giving way to younger, stronger forces.

1935: You are forced (with money) to retire.
It becomes evident that the only way to get older workers to leave the job market is to pay them so much that they can't say no. Even so, most retirees wish they could work. Doing nothing is hard. Approximately 25 per cent of retirees start their own businesses. Eleanor Roosevelt is running more campaigns in collaboration with the healthcare industry to convince the populace that old means weak and tired. She wants them to know that they deserve a few good years before they kick the bucket. They 'deserve' to retire. This idea spreads to the rest of the industrialized countries. Retirement – because you're worth it!

The Second World War: And now they want you back.
Young men are sent to war, and there is a shortage of labour. Everyone is now supposed to join the workforce: women, old, children. You are sucked back into the job market. Due to wage-freezing, private companies introduce pensions to attract labour. The nastier companies, of course, speculate in never paying them out; the seeds are sown for the welfare reforms of trade unions and political parties.

1950: Live strong, die young.
The average lifespan of an industrial worker falls to 44. Their life is hard, dirty, dangerous and brutal. For the women, it is worse.

1955: You tie your kids to a flagpole.
The tractor makes 1 million (25 per cent) Danes unemployed. You move from the rural areas to the city and bring horses, pigs, cows and sheep. Day care is for the wealthy, so while you work, you tie a leash to your little ones so they can

play at a safe distance from traffic. You need to get used to something completely new, namely 'leisure time'. And with it also the idea that the last phase of life is no longer about death preparation, but can be a reward for all your blood, sweat and tears.

The 1970s: Youth rebellion, the old white man begins to falter.
Now all of a sudden young people are rebellious. They jump around in front of you in the media, stealing your thunder, they knock down walls, break boundaries, mix everything up, smoke weed and play the guitar. They make old people seem *really* old.

The 1980s: Individualization and 'a new freedom'.
Hey! There is something called spaghetti. And red wine and olive oil and holidays in the sun. The children have moved away from home, you have some good money, the house has been insulated, and for the first time in history, you are no longer afraid of starvation. You are more fearful of not having lived. You hear yourself say, 'Oh, I am soooo looking forward to retiring.' However, leaving the labour market still feels a bit cross-border. But hey, there is a house in Spain to visit, and a golf course to join.

The 1990s: It goes completely haywire.
Everyone is entitled to a huge kitchen. And a new car. And an extended vacation. And a cute hat and a pricey bag. Pension becomes passion. Is it one to three years, and then it's over? No, no. Now is the time for passion, doing what you have postponed while drinking red wine and devouring books and experiences. The seniors are rebranded as either 'enjoyers of life' or 'resourceless and weak'. Their nightmare becomes

being handed over to the cold hands of the system, where the food is bland, and everything smells like pee.

The pension companies seem to be only interested in the rich. They develop solutions to get the elderly and their big money to bring even higher returns. More, bigger, fatter is the mantra of this era. The big taboo of this age group is that they think they are socially minded. But they are used to 'society' fixing it. So the wealthy elderly sympathize with the poor elderly – but they do not lift a finger to change the situation.

The oos: Financial crisis and anxiety.
The world's economic dominoes fall and reveal how flimsy designed society is. Politics has become too big for the small problems, and too small for the big ones. Politics is almost only about resource allocation and behaviour control, based on the tribalistic premise that there is not enough. No one has trained to be able to create visions and design radical experiments. So to control you, you are constantly told that you must stay in your corner (the old dusty corner). You should be afraid – the world is dangerous. If you think you can do without the old political parties, the trade union movement and the classic retirement savings, you are an asocial, couch-surfing, gut-wrenching troublemaker. Nothing can be solved without new forms of co-operation, but the elite dare not let go. They therefore appear even more worldly and elitist, and people withdraw from traditional solutions.

You have become accustomed to a certain standard of living, and you start to see that life is quite long. And old age – maybe – is not as unpleasant as you had expected. Perhaps you can grow old AND, at the same time, tougher, wiser and more energetic. And maybe it's not too late to become a supermodel...

10s: Strictly Come Dancing and MasterChef.

The world is an incredibly complicated place. And we easily get scared and apathetic. But what you did yesterday doesn't work any more, and you know you have to try something new. The older you get, the less BS you are willing to take – the rebellion lies just under the surface. Like having an attitude about things. Saying no and standing your ground. Not doing as 'you should', choosing your own media channels, switching off your mobile and starting to feel life. You find that you love watching people succeed on TV – when they dance and bake or live on a farm and do everything themselves. Ordinary people can do much more than they thought when given the right framework. Maybe that could be me too, you think. Perhaps there are brand-new ways to go? Maybe I should master something new? And surround myself with some new, cool friends?

THE FUTURE: RISE OF THE REBELS

The 'rebels' are just around the corner. Because you are fed up with all the bureaucratic BS and standard solutions that don't work. Because you see others succeed in their ideas and because the world has never been as rich in opportunities as it is now. Because you're probably *getting* older, but not *feeling* old. You're not scared any more. You see the future as it comes and meet it, not full of concerns but with vitality, curiosity and willingness to experiment.

Co-creation and crowdfunding will become a typical way of developing solutions. New generations learn financial housekeeping at school, and an ideal graduation gift is a membership in a FIRE training group (Financially Independent, Retire Early, where you learn to become financially independent before you turn 30). Steady employment is for the few – everyone else works as freelancers, on projects, as temps, or is self-employed. In many jobs, there is a battle to get the best gig, but few need to work from morning to evening. We orient ourselves towards the 'village' – the resilient local community where we look out for each other. The municipality is no longer a building but a feeling. 'Work' is also helping each other as volunteers in the local area. We are rewarded more for doing the right thing. Sick or unhealthy people are rewarded for exercising, being a good citizen, studying and experimenting with what they have to offer.

The classic retirement scheme has brought us far. But now it needs to take a break. Before it breaks us. It gave us 'more life'. Now it is up to us to make it better. Let's do that with great responsibility for both our own and others' happiness.

PART FOUR

Me, Myself and AI

Now that technological advances have seemingly bestowed humanity with the power of the gods – the ability to create artificial intelligence virtually indistinguishable from the 'real thing' – even the ultimate goal of immortality (or amortality – that is, immortal aside from accidental or violent causes) does not seem nearly as far-fetched as it did decades ago.

Our mastering of weird and wonderful mind-and-body-altering science can be summed up by the transhumanist movement's manifesto, which basically states that *we can and should eradicate human suffering and ageing as a cause of death by utilizing whatever technology we have at our disposal* – be it cognitive enhancement devices and brain-machine interfaces, mind-altering drugs, cyborg body parts, cryogenics, biohacking, or even young-blood transfusions (as Dion Chang describes in Chapter 18) – to augment our bodies and our minds.

In other words, the transhumanist goal is to live long and prosper. And who can argue that this is indeed a noble objective.

However, even noble ends sometimes require terrible means. Utopian ideals all too often tend to cause untold suffering to those trampled upon along the way or left out of the promised kingdom altogether. As we master control over life and death, new conflicts and competition for scarce resources will most assuredly emerge. As always, the dichotomy between freedom to self-actualize and equality and fraternity threatens to fracture humanity, potentially into entirely different species as we look further down the line. Just like with the economic struggle between liberty and equality, it is going to become hard to accommodate both natural selection and intelligent design.

As intelligently designed embryos and DIY cyborg body and brain enhancements become commercially available and socially acceptable, parents could eventually become *obligated* to genetically engineer their own offspring (governments have a history of dabbling in eugenics). Either that, or doom their unaltered carbon descendants to, at best, poverty and irrelevance, and at worst oppression, or even slavery or extermination in a world where intelligently designed and technologically enhanced super humans could feasibly have every advantage – height, health, attractiveness, even intelligence – over their naturally selected counterparts (as Craig Wing explains in Chapter 20).

The economic inequality and xenophobia that already threatens to fracture human civilization is nothing compared to the biological and technological inequality we are sleepwalking into.

In this section, our authors explore what happens as humanity transcends our biological and cognitive limits and begins to grasp beyond our reach towards superintelligence and super-longevity. Here, we encourage you to look even further into the future and reflect on the ultimate ends we are working towards as we begin to become our own gods.

16

Back to the Future (of Ourselves)

by Cathy Hackl, futurist, technologist and VR specialist

We have managed to digitize our personalities, our payments, our education and even how we find our soulmates, but as the era of 'spatial computing' is dawning, our physical and digital lives are starting to truly blend seamlessly together. We are at the cusp of a new reality where who we are as humans will become a central question and the decisions we make today will impact our world for centuries to come. When the stakes are so high, what will identity mean in the future?

Mention the future and people usually think of movies. Some are an example of unbridled tech and uncontrolled growth. *The Circle* is one example. In the name of accountability, cameras watch and record everyone, everywhere. (This leads to its own questions about Big Tech and its impact on our lives, digital and real.)

There's *In Time*, where everyone has an augmented countdown running on their arm. When the time runs out, you die. People are paid in time and can trade time by touching arms. A class system keeps some constantly watching the clock while others live in luxury, seemingly forever.

In *Ready Player One*, the metaverse (the virtual reality where society works, plays and goes to school) is threatened by paywalls and intrusive ads blocking every step of the way. It looks like a mock-up of an augmented reality grocery store[114] that has neon lights, signs and pop-ups that are so distracting it makes you want to turn your phone off. UX designers everywhere cringe.

Movies are just movies. They're entertainment. They're thought experiments as to what humanity will be like in the future. They sometimes give us a small glimpse or hint into where we are headed as humanity continues to augment itself using technology.

In a way, technology and humanity shouldn't go together. Technology is built on rules and if-then statements. It's designed not to make mistakes. Apps look pretty and are simple enough for anyone to use.

Humans are the complete opposite. We make mistakes. In fact, we need to make mistakes to learn. We break rules. We're messy and complicated.

Despite these differences, humans and technology seem to work together. Phones have become an extension of our hands. Smart devices are another persona to talk to. Our online profiles take on a whole new personality and we now have one identity in real life and another in the digital world.

In an effort to provide an identity check, phones give us screen time reports. We take digital detoxes and announce

---

[114]Keiichi Matsuda, 'Hyper Reality', 19 May 2016, YouTube Available from:https://www.youtube.com/watch?v=YJg02ivYzSs

social media breaks. We battle distracted parenting while trying to set a good example of technology use for our kids, only later to have to battle with them to put down their devices at the dinner table.

We've managed to digitize our lives in ways that humans never needed to or wanted to in the past. Our virtual and physical realities are converging even further and the decisions we make now carry with them very high stakes. So, when the stakes are so high, what does it mean to be human in the 2020s and beyond? What will identity mean in the future?

VIRTUAL IDENTITY

Fortnite, which has become a hit around the world, is a video game but its parent company, Epic, sees it as more than that. They see it as a pathway into the future of what the Internet will become. Not too long ago, they started holding concerts in *Fortnite* and most recently, Travis Scott's *Fortnite* concert,[115] Astronomical, drew in close to 28 million gamers and viewers into a virtual event like no other.

What this concert showed was *Fortnite*'s own transformation. It's not a game any more. It's a universe where players shop, play, fight and rock out to concerts. *Fortnite* didn't just reimagine what a concert could be. They strategically built their world with history, layers and depth. They realized the next evolution of the Internet. It's the metaverse where people interact with the environment and each other. It has its own rules (or possible lack thereof), laws of physics and culture.

[115]Cathy Hackl, 'Toward the Metaverse: What Fortnite's Latest Concert Tells Us About the Future of Virtual Presence', LinkedIn, 14 May 2020. Available from: www.linkedin.com/pulse/toward-metaverse-what-fortnites-latest-concert-tells-us-cathy-hackl/

This transition has kicked off further interest from artists, politicians and the entertainment industry towards accelerating their virtual presence, campaigns and IP. The concert showed that you don't have to be in full virtual reality (although that doesn't hurt) to feel immersed in another world.

The Travis Scott concert took place in *Fortnite* in part because of COVID-19. Concerts aren't the only virtual presence accelerated by the coronavirus.

Esports are another example of the acceleration of virtual presence. Esports too have slowly been gaining speed over the years but as COVID-19 lockdowns kept fans from stadiums, real athletes turned to gaming. One example is *The Race*. Real Formula 1[116] and Indianapolis 500 drivers took to the virtual track with simulators. People who never had an interest in esports before suddenly wanted to be involved.

Virtual presence isn't something we have to force people into. It's a natural progression of the technology we have. It doesn't have to be a shallow social media experience. People are finding social-rich ways to interact with each other in virtual spaces. As long as we can continue to put people first, virtual realities have a chance to be a different kind of internet. One free of ad-first revenue models. Hopefully, we can set that as the tone for the rest of identity technology in the future.

The best virtual presences are ones that can be built upon and continue to grow for decades to come. Museums bring artefacts to your home with augmented reality.[117] Augmented

[116]Alan Baldwin, 'Virtual world races to fill sporting void left by Ccoronavrirus', World Economic Forum, 22 March 2020. Available from: www.weforum.org/agenda/2020/03/virtual-world-races-to-fill-sporting-void-left-by-coronavirus

[117]Barbara Bridgers, 'Bring an Island Deity to Life with Augmented Reality', Art Del Mar exhibition, Met Museum, 15 May 2020. Available from: www.metmuseum.org/blogs/collection-insights/2020/augmented-reality-zemi-arte-del-mar

reality and virtual spaces are put to the test as educators and co-workers push their boundaries to continue teaching and working despite not making it to the office or classroom.

BRAIN–MACHINE INTERFACES
AND AUGMENTED HUMANS

Brain–machine interfaces (BMI) are another example of how technology does and will enhance humans. Brain–machine interfaces were initially developed to restore motor function in paralysed patients. They can also affect mood by restoring emotion in people who have neuropsychiatric disorders.

With a BMI, you can control robots with just a thought. By installing microelectrodes and recording devices on the brain, brain–machine interfaces can translate brain electrical activity via a computer to send a robot into motion (like an electronic arm).

Elon Musk, however, envisions a different use for BMIs than only medical research. He is building his own brain–machine interface called the Neuralink. Musk imagines a future where everyone has a Neuralink embedded on their brains. The Neuralink lets people connect to devices with their minds. He even sees it as a way to stop humans from being outpaced by artificial intelligence.[118]

AI can become our therapists and our doctors. Tell your doctor you diagnosed yourself on WebMD today and they might laugh. But in the future WebMD may just become one, personified official medical source powered by artificial

[118]Charlotte Edwards, 'Elon Musk's "disease curing" Neuralink human brain implants could be ready "within a year"', The Sun, 8 May 2020. Available from: www.thesun.co.uk/tech/11578395/disease-curing-neuralink-human-brain-implant-could-be-ready-within-a-year-says-elon-musk/

intelligence and represented by an avatar. If the Neuralink can help doctors to process more information, faster, while still with a human touch and creativity, then brain–machine interfaces may be the answer.

On the flip side, the Neuralink might make humans lose some of their natural brainpower. We used to be able to recall the phone numbers of all our friends. Now we depend on our phones. Some argue that people have lost a sense of spatial awareness with the advent of Google Maps.

From personal experience, having tried several external BMI devices from companies like Neurable, Neurosity and NextMind, I've been able to change channels and dim lights using just my thoughts, or input a code with my brain in a VR escape room of sorts, or even scroll my iPad using just my mind while cooking at home. These experiences have been transformative, and I'd be lying if I said that my brain doesn't light up every time I think of using BMI. It's like my brain really wants the workout.

RISE OF AVATARS AND VIRTUAL HUMANS

Every social media and phone company has their own version of an avatar. There are Facebook avatars, Apple Memojis, Samsung AR Emojis and Bitmoji.

Currently, avatars are pretty basic and somewhat cartoony. They come in preset poses or use our cameras to copy our mouth or body movements. Looking into the future, avatars have the capability to be much more. Enabled with artificial intelligence, our avatars will know how we act, what we say, what we like and don't like, and who we most like to interact with. You might not know the difference if you're talking to your friend or their avatar online.

Instead of having the constant pressure to post, comment and engage online, we can have our avatars do the work for us. Our avatars can report back to us through a brain–machine interface the highlights from the day (or hour) so we can step in, if needed.

Avatars can do more than help manage our online profiles. They can be the bridge between our humanity and virtual humans.

Virtual humans, once relegated to the background of movies, are now taking centre stage. One such account is Lil Miquela,[119] a forever 19-year-old girl who joined Instagram in 2016. She now has over two million followers, a music deal, and multiple sponsors.

With her perfect looks and fashion sense, one might wonder: are advertising companies grooming us for AI with sexy robot girls or is there something more to Lil Miquela and her friends? Maybe they'll become self-aware and leave us like the AI did in the movie *Her*. Or maybe they'll continue the next trend of advertising by tricking younger generations into unrealistic beauty standards and accomplishments. Not a model/singer/songwriter/actress by 19 years old? Better give up now. It's hard to find the silver lining behind an Instagram robot that's groomed by a whole marketing team.

That's where our own avatars can come in. Social media is a place where everyone feels like they need to post the most perfect version of themselves. People (especially teenagers) take hundreds of photos of themselves just to edit and post the perfect one to Instagram. Now with perfect robot teenagers to compete with, the pressure is too much. Avatars could be the answer to online presence by letting us enjoy reality.

[119]Instagram. Available from: Miquela (@lilmiquela) • Instagram photos and videos

Not to mention the clothes. Fashion is getting a redesign with augmented and virtual upgrades. We already dress our Bitmojis to match our moods or personal styles. Now we can virtually dress ourselves in clothes we might not be able to afford in real life. The Fabricant, Dapper Labs and artist Johanna Jaskowska sold a virtual dress for $9,500.[120] To some, a $9,500 virtual dress is ludicrous. But looking forward, it makes sense. No one wants to be stuck wearing the same clothes all the time, even if it's a virtual version of themselves. Even Lil Miquela's fans are tired of her virtual hair always being up in buns.

Digital clothes don't have to follow the laws of physics. We can change them instantly to match our moods or how we want to be portrayed. We can take 'dress for the job you want' to the next level, since many of us are transitioning to virtual work.

SYNTHETIC ROBOTS

In the future, if you ask someone what it means to be human, they might tell you to be human is to be a cyborg. Synthetic body replacements, genetic testing, robot eyeballs and retinas – these will all be a natural part of what it means to be human.

Sanctuary AI, maker of synthetic robots, sees their human-looking robots as a force for good. The company envisions robots doing the jobs people might not want to. For instance, taking care of the elderly and being their companion. My friend Suzanne Gildert, CEO of Sanctuary

[120]Jon Fingas, 'A digital "dress" sold for $9,500', Engadget, 27 May 2019. Available from: www.engadget.com/2019-05-27-fabricant-blockchain-digital-dress.html

AI, thinks of robots not as machines, but as the 'ultimate self-portrait'.[121] She hopes humans will think about the 'kind of "robot rights" superintelligent machines may need once they start to make their way into offices and society as a whole'.

This leads to the question, why are we thinking about robot rights and their identities when we seem to be designing away our own? Who will we be when humanoid robots are doing our jobs (physical and knowledge-based)? Virtual humans rule the Internet with their perfect looks and auto-tuned voices. And we attach our own brains to the Neuralink.

We can create robots, train them, and build in our biases as to what it means to be human. But who is to say robots, virtual humans and our avatars may wake up one day to their own individualism? At the end of the day, robots are not human. But our desire to be more than human might make us more robotic.

IN THE FUTURE...

Will we end up assimilating like the Borg in *Star Trek* or will we still be able to keep our flaws? Maybe robots and virtual humans will be a reminder of our greater humanity as people. Despite our merging identities with computers, we can continue as creators, inventors and futurists. Perhaps, in the future, being a completely authentic human being will be a novelty.

---

[121]Shane Schick, 'Sanctuary AI founder is making robots that are exact human replicas (starting with herself)', B2B News Network, 23 October 2018. Available from: www.b2bnn.com/2018/10/sanctuary-ai-robotics/

Whichever way we go, it's important to remember that technology itself isn't inherently good or bad. It's how we use it. What starts out as good intentions can turn into unchecked tech. If we can keep in mind the lessons we're learning today about human and technology identity, we can make the best choices for the generations after us. The stakes for the future of humanity are high.

17

Artificial Intelligence versus Natural Reasoning

by Steven Marlow, leading technologist focused on behaviourism, cognition, the philosophy of other minds, and the future of the thinking machine

Why don't we all get along? Conflict narratives between humans and AI set the wrong tone for the future. The future of scientific efforts shouldn't be restricted to the seeds sown in childhood fiction. Stories with grave hardship against a seemingly superior adversary always end when some fatal flaw is uncovered, and it's usually a barrier that a child could overcome.

MY FUTURE DEFINED

People write stories about a future that is often based on some current trend, or past event, with a personal message layered on top. While a lot of effort might go into building a familiar world, because it needs to be relatable to the reader, often the 'new content' feels like something that has been mentioned before. It's a kind of remix paradox, where imagination is constrained by current knowledge, and the boundary can only expand when you push at it repeatedly. We need to be exposed to the strange and unfamiliar until it is no longer strange, and no longer unfamiliar. This is my take on futurism. Finding those boundaries and making those concepts part of our general understanding.

My personal spin on what is otherwise just more speculation on the future of artificial intelligence actually mirrors the biggest problem in AI research. How can we present a new idea that isn't already tied to a popular notion of what AI and robots are supposed to be like? How does any conversation or philosophy lead into unexplored areas? How can a system that operates under a fixed set of rules ever have the freedom to step beyond them?

THE STORIES WE TELL

We write about the futures we want, but it's usually a projection of some experience or belief, rather than a crystal ball into the world of tomorrow. Stories do have a way of guiding society, if only because there is a shared reference point for a large number of people to talk about (the water cooler of fictitious dreams). This directed activity results in moving technology and society forward, and people can look back and say, yes, this new thing is a version of what people used to write about. What we don't see or hear about are the things that have failed.

Well, that isn't exactly true, because asking 'where are my flying cars and jetpacks?' has become a meme. The actual failure is in not letting go of some ideas. Just because someone writes about a magical way to teleport characters in a story from a ship in orbit to the planet surface, to move the story along quickly doesn't mean such a technology is within the realm of what's physically possible. I'm not saying we can't dream, but if you are going to use science to make a thing, then please use that same science when being critical of it.

All of the dreams and all of the stories surely keep us entertained, and do provide something to aim for, but is that what really shapes our future? We are living in the future, from the perspective of someone in the 1950s, but it just feels like more of the same. The changes have been too small and gradual to really notice. The really big ideas are still just that, ideas. And if they haven't been completely debunked, what's holding us back? Is the pace of change outside of our control?

Despite our aspirations and hyperconnected society, we human animals are still operating from a village clan mentality that goes back thousands of years. The best description I can give is that we have domesticated ourselves, and the animal nature is always right there under the surface. Dream as we might, it's our waking lives that contain complex interactions and a kind of social mass that is resistive to our individual ideas. The only counter to our group animal behaviour is introducing something that is equally large. Something that can also take on a life of its own. The way in which our species deals with non-human entities also lacks a degree of development that could hamper the introduction of our 'robotic kin'.

THE NARRATIVE POINTS TO ITSELF

We tell ourselves stories where the goal is to overcome some kind of adversity. In science fiction, the presence of super-smart machines (or aliens) with some critical flaw we can exploit in the end gives us a sense of comfort. The fact that all of the super-smart machines we write about have issues in the first place is actually the point of this chapter.

There is a disconnect between the kinds of tools we are building today and this false impression of what those tools can do. It's not easy to untangle, but the short version is that the public's collective consciousness has been primed to understand AI in a very specific way. This language of understanding is used in two very bad ways. The first is to abuse it by selling the idea of 'the future is here' when in fact the software and accomplishments have less to do with progress of AI in the last 60 years, and almost everything to do with the advancements in computing power.

The second, and more recent, issue is how the general understanding of what AI can do gets used as a punchbag to cover for the dumb systems that people really need to be focused on. The left hand is building a statistical model to assist judges in setting jail times, while the right is in a bare-knuckle fight over driverless cars making moral decisions. That very real algorithm has limits that result in lengthy jail times for people who don't deserve it. The unreal moral agent has an even longer list of technical limits, but it's a better story for the media to write about. This gives it a wider audience, which leads to a wider understanding (even if false), and inevitably a wider market in which to sell. More stories get more clicks. More people are sharing more opinions.

The impression most people have of AI comes from science fiction, and it's more than just a selling point for a product's potential. Every other week there is an article about AI being used to 'create' music or 'invent' a new medical drug. People are encouraged to marvel at the ability of such advances that give computers the power to do things that are getting closer and closer to human abilities. However, human minds remain an integral part of the loop. They collect the input data, build the systems, and interpret the results using knowledge and intuition that current machines are no closer to demonstrating than they were 60 years ago.

How do you get people to unlearn that kind of story? You can explain that the technology required to operate at this mystical level of predictive performance is still decades away, and that some of the assessments involved can only be done in hindsight. I've had to say it many times that cars on the road today, operating in 'autonomous' mode, have failed to even apply the brakes before a crash. Why are we even asking how they should act based on the life history of passengers in another car or crossing an intersection? Brake, and swerve if you can. In the few seconds before any accident, this is the extent of our human abilities. Slamming on the brakes and then trying to steer is so innate that technology had to be developed to prevent the front wheels from skidding across the road, so that, even under hard braking, we could maintain some control over the vehicle's direction.

THE ALL-SEEING AI

That's actually another issue with trying to wrap fictional AI abilities around complex, but ultimately dumb systems. Foresight, time travel, or pre-crime levels of awareness. Current tools only have access to a subset of the information we might use to make a decision. They have an advantage in terms of quantity of data, but we sacrifice a lot of privacy for iffy improvements. No amount of data will allow current systems to see into the future. Knowing what will happen with a degree of certainty sounds great if you are selling a product or service, but it's just statistics and probabilities, not AI.

It's remarkable that humans are so unaware of how unaware we are from moment to moment. The world around us just feels like one complete space, but information is only being updated a few times a second, and not even in an efficient way (I'm referring to conscious awareness, but 'raw' perception might be system-limited to a few hundred samples per second). An image processing program can compare two images of the same room, with only two or three minor things altered, and pick out the anomalies right away. Humans will walk past the same object we've been trying to find for five minutes before it finally jumps out at us.

What we see with Big Data is trying to find the patterns we would never find, or, in the case of many biases, something that was right in front of us the whole time. It's an effort to use more data, not less, to make sense of the world. For self-driving cars, it's a sensor fusion problem. The human ability to ignore non-critical information does lead to blind spots, and accidents, but a 360-degree view and hyper-accurate data on the distance and speed of other objects is worthless to an AI that has no understanding of what all those points of data really mean.

It's an issue of representation. You understand the different patterns as cars along the road, and trees, and a child playing in the driveway. There is a deep relationship between these objects, and an understanding about them that you don't have to explicitly run through as you notice them. Current technology just reduces everything into disconnected binary data, LOTS of it, and tries to find some kind of link between all of the 1s and 0s, rather than accepting a more analogue abstraction. That used to be the way.

Since AI is used as a blanket label for the different forms of deep learning, it's become popular to move the 'deeper human abilities' into AGI (artificial general intelligence). It's closely aligned with the original goals of AI from the late 1950s (good old-fashioned AI) and with public perceptions of what AI is supposed to be. Unfortunately, the community is so divided over methods and explanations of the problems being addressed that they tend to point towards the same end goal but with diverging pathways. It might boil down to a representation problem, or how such information about the world is constructed within machine space.

Humans don't 'transmit' general knowledge to each other. If I'm giving you directions to a place in a city you have never visited before, I don't have to include detailed instructions of how traffic lights work, or what parking is. When people talk about AGI, this is the aspect they should focus on. What is the lowest amount of common knowledge a human may need to survive in the world? Compare what an eighth-grader knows to that of a hamster. A mostly conscious being versus an animal that is good with tunnels and OK with spinning a wheel. Although with this example, where the animal doesn't even reach the level of general intelligence, it still has a better grasp upon the geometry of objects and the physical world around it than the most advanced AI of today.

KEEP THE DREAM ALIVE

There are a lot of people working in AI or AI-related fields, but does everyone have to work on the next search engine, social media site or data collection app? I don't even see it as AI research any more, but shouting 'machine learning!' at my Twitter feed isn't really effective. And I've been saying AI many times myself when 'deep neural networks' or 'reinforcement learning' would have been more accurate.

I don't want to be completely cynical and say that marketing ruins everything, but the groundwork that went into defining the AI narrative is being used to push non-AI technology, which at the very least is eroding all of the public's goodwill.

Why do people buy smart speakers and voice assistants? The better question might be, how many of those people stop using the latest techno gadget after only a few weeks, and why. For some, the novelty wears off, and it has no day-to-day practical use. In the other direction, a lot of people will (intentionally or not) prop the device up by helping it along. They are getting more out of their ownership than the tech can provide. In both cases, expectations have not been met. Rather than circling back to the fictional AI narratives and overhyped sales pitch stuff again, it's important we examine the interplay of technical feasibility with design goals.

The same fictional ideas that drive people's imaginations also drive the aspirations of those working on that next social robot. Both sides can relate to each other using a common language, but if we look at AI as a science, well, there is not enough science there for us to work with. Milestones and publicity stunts are great for building a brand or reputation, but so much of the work still requires explicit coding of some kind (human intelligence that goes into the design of a system, crafting of how the interactions will happen, or just farming out the selling point of AI; manual review).

What the designers promise is not always a bit of fibbing because, often, they really do believe their goal can be accomplished. Should they know better? Maybe they become aware of the limits, or the gap between what they can code, what data can be processed, and how boxed-in the final product is going to be. Is it at the level of a public works project, like an AI to nowhere? Humans, given a short time to interact with an AI, basically start from the same level of assessment afforded to other humans. The longer a device can go without breaking our expectations, or the longer it can maintain the illusion of 'fully functional', the more praise we have for its abilities.

Machine learning of today can't come close to people's expectations. It is a narrow radio tower supported by guidelines. If you push back against the AI 'industry' you're met with claims that a few algorithms can not only simulate human interactions, but even reach a level of actual human reasoning (so don't start mentioning robot rights or suggesting that an AI could have agency!). It's rooted in how the technical aspects are framed, as connectionism or reductionism. It's like trying to build an entire car while being hyper-focused on tyres.

In drafting this chapter, my initial concept was how tech is just a tool, and that humans are always going to be the bad actors (and make note of my objection to regulating the research into better AI). Not even halfway into a first draft, I was being nagged by the issue of framing and the kind of stories that people tell. This became a message about what I want, and where it should lead, rather than just another rant about 'not my AI' and the downward spiral of data consumption that shapes the industry today. A harshly written letter to a few billionaire CEOs isn't going to have an impact on anyone. Better that I tell a story, and expand the boundaries of the ongoing conversation. Others may be encouraged to tell a similar story, and that slowly shapes a greater appreciation for actual advancements.

18

Keeping Up With The Cadavers

by Dion Chang, futurist, trend analyst and founder of Flux Trends. Many people dream of living longer. Dion Chang doesn't share that dream and encourages us to consider the reality of living well beyond our 'sell-by' date

Whether you're searching for immortality, or simply amortality, you're essentially trying to hack the natural order of evolutionary biology. Science has managed to make great strides, medically, by limiting or eliminating life-threatening diseases. With this 'new' quest for amortality, the lines between eradicating disease for a healthier life and living longer as a vanity project are becoming blurred. This creates a fork in the road, and we need to decide which route to take.

The 1992 film *Death Becomes Her* revolves around two rivals both seeking eternal youth so that they can outperform the other in both their personal and professional lives. They discover an elixir of eternal life and their bodies are restored to a youthful vibrancy as they embrace the promise of perpetuity.

Ironically, while they are able to live forever, their physical bodies are unable to withstand wear and tear, so they become progressively battered and torn, leading them to depend upon one another for repair work for the rest of eternity.

There's a cautionary tale in there for all those in search of living longer or even forever, especially the wealthy techpreneurs in Silicon Valley who, in the last few years, have poured eye-watering amounts of money into research that might lead to slowing or stopping the ageing process. Messing with our mortality will come with unintended consequences.

While the concept might seem appealing, the road to amortality is filled with complications: jarring potholes like overpopulation, finite planetary resources, climate change and how to budget for a never-ending life.

Thanks to improved diets and living conditions, our life expectancies have steadily increased over the past centuries. For example, at the beginning of the 20th century the average life expectancy in America hovered around 49. Today, the average baby born in America will live to approximately 79, with the average 35-year-old living to around 80, and the average 65-year-old making it to at least 83.[122]

In the last century especially, scientific research has led to vastly improved healthcare and disease control, resulting in sharp increases in life expectancies around the world. The primary aim of doctors and scientists has always been to try to maintain physical well-being, prevent illness and eradicate diseases.

But humans are a greedy lot.

[122]David Leonhardt, 'Life Expectancy Data', *New York Times*, 27 September 2006. Available from: www.nytimes.com/2006/09/27/business/27leonhardt_sidebar.html

For many, it's no longer enough to simply live a healthy and fulfilled life, and accept that your time is over when your body naturally reaches its sell-by date.

This is the natural order of evolutionary biology. We are designed to die.

But in Silicon Valley a movement is under way with attempts to 'hack' the human body and the natural order of life.

THE SCIENTIFIC INTERVENTION

Around 2013, a group of very prominent (and very wealthy) techpreneurs[123] in Silicon Valley started to invest in new companies with a primary objective of dodging or delaying death.[124] Leading the pack are Google's co-founders Sergey Brin and Larry Page, who have both made substantial investments in setting up the biotech company Calico Labs, which then became a subsidiary of Alphabet in 2015. The primary mandate of Calico is to work – long-term – on understanding the causes of ageing and put an end to them.

The team of scientists at Calico are pooled from varied fields of medicine, drug development, molecular biology, genetics and computational biology. According to their website, Calico aims to 'devise interventions that enable people to lead longer and healthier lives'. All well and good, but peel back the layers and the ripple effect, and growing obsession for amortality starts to surface.

---

[123]'Immortality is the new IT: Tech moguls chase longevity', Times of India, 9 October 2017. Available from: timesofindia.indiatimes.com/home/science/immortality-is-the-new-it-tech-moguls-chase-longevity/articleshow/61005318.cms

[124]Laura Lorenzetti, 'The Obsession With "Curing" Aging Is Now Big Business', *Entrepreneur*, 7 March 2016. Available from: www.entrepreneur.com/slideshow/272057

Bill Maris, the founder of Calico, has in turn also made investments in other companies that aim to slow ageing, improve longevity and possibly reverse disease. He places both his money and his confidence behind these developments. As he said in an interview with Bloomberg Markets, 'If you ask me today, is it possible to live to be 500? The answer is yes.'

Sergey Brin, however, has a more ambitious goal. He hopes to someday 'cure death'.

The lure of amortality is obviously a powerful one, especially if you have money to burn. Many of the companies who have joined the quest are interlinked, making the Silicon Valley 'VC [venture capital] amortality club' a close-knit, wealthy and very powerful cabal.

Other techpreneurs who have joined the 'VC amortality club' include:

- Mark Zuckerberg, who co-sponsors (with Sergey Brin) a $33 million Breakthrough Prize in Life Sciences, which focuses on curing age-related diseases.
  (The prize encourages breakthroughs in specific fields like genetics, molecular biology, oncology and neurology to better understand how cells and organs function to help fight some of the most deadly diseases.)
- Amazon founder Jeff Bezos, who has invested approximately $116 million into Unity Biotechnology, another Silicon Valley anti-ageing firm that aims to eliminate many chronic age-related ailments for good, such as mitochondrial dysfunction.
  (Mitochondria exist within all cells in our bodies and are crucial to energy conversion as well as immunity against invading organisms such as viruses, bacteria and parasites.)

- Peter Thiel, co-founder of PayPal (and Google investor), who has a more 'modest' goal. He just wants to live to be 120 years old. He is hedging his bets and has invested millions into approximately 14 health and biotech companies trying to make that happen. Most notable is his $3.5 million donation to anti-ageing researcher Aubrey de Grey to start the Methuselah Foundation, a non-profit focused on exploring life-extension therapies.

  (The Methuselah Prize has been designed to encourage scientists to work on anti-ageing research and treat ageing as a 'medical condition'. David Gobel, 63, who co-founded the Methuselah Foundation with Aubrey de Grey, is known for popularizing the idea of 'longevity escape velocity', a hypothetical situation in which life expectancy grows faster than time passes. So, essentially, the first 1,000-year-old could be only 10 years younger than the first 150-year-old. Gobel says the organization's aim is to make '90 the new 50 by 2030'.)

Benchmarking what you think your amortality project might achieve by a certain year is risky, especially if you announce it to the media. Take, for example, Russian entrepreneur Dmitry Itskov (who aims to live for 10,000 years). His amortality project, the 2045 Initiative (aka the Avatar Project), launched in 2013, mapped out a four-stage plan to dodge death, and would culminate in replacing the need for a body altogether – by 2045.

- Avatar A will be achieved with the creation of a robot that can be controlled by our brain.
- Avatar B will be achieved when a brain can be transplanted to a synthetic body.

- Avatar C will be achieved after the contents of a person's brain can be uploaded into a synthetic one.
- The project will end with Avatar D – the creation of a hologram that will replace bodies completely.

Avatar A, which was envisaged to materialize between 2015 and 2020, has yet to become a reality.

Yuval Noah Harari has also deflated the hopes and aspirations of Larry Page and Sergey Brin. In his book *Homo Deus,* he mentions specifically that Calico won't be able to develop a cure to prevent ageing in time to save both Google co-founders. But this hasn't stopped the funding.

BUT WHAT DRIVES THESE TECHPRENEURS TO POUR MILLIONS INTO AMORTALITY RESEARCH?

In the case of the Google co-founders, Larry Page and Sergey Brin, the quest is personal. Both are racing against time. Page has Hashimoto's thyroiditis disease, also known as chronic lymphocytic thyroiditis, an autoimmune disease in which the thyroid gland is gradually destroyed, while Brin carries a genetic mutation that makes him vulnerable to Parkinson's disease.

Peter Thiel and Larry Ellison (co-founder of Oracle) are in it, it seems, merely to stall the inevitable. The main focus of their investments is anti-ageing (although Thiel has a more diversified portfolio that includes 3D printing of organs and human genomics). At the time of writing, Thiel is 53 years old and Ellison 76 years old, and Ellison has been quoted as saying, 'Death has never made any sense to me. How can a person be there and then just vanish, just not be there?'

One tech billionaire who has been vocal in his objection to all this money being thrown at amortality research is Bill

Gates. He has branded the notion of the wealthy techpreneurs seeking amortality as 'egocentric' and has questioned why this money is not being spent on helping people currently living with life-threatening diseases.

In the aftermath of the COVID-19 pandemic, many will be asking the same.

THE SOCIAL RIPPLE EFFECT

Currently, there is a growing trend for delayed parenting, driven by women who don't necessarily 'want it all' (at the same time) but prefer to 'try it all' (i.e. a fulfilling career as well as motherhood, which does not necessarily overlap). Financial services companies are already flagging this as a problematic bottleneck that will occur later in life, when saving for retirement collides with putting your kids through university. If our lifespans stretch beyond 120 years, then how does one plan financially for that extended future?

Amortality, rather than immortality, would still have a time limit. You would live longer, and hopefully maintain a relatively healthy, youthful exuberance during that extension period, but the cost of age-extending drugs and therapies will not come cheap. So not only will you have to deal with an extended income stream to feed your further delayed retirement, but your medical bills will grow exponentially.

We might be able to find a way to live longer, but we have yet to find a way to completely stop the ageing process, so in essence you will work longer and pay more to maintain amortality, as well as – eventually – the bottleneck of mounting medical bills (whether covered by yourself or a national health insurance scheme, these life-extending treatments do not come cheap) – when your body finally succumbs to its unnatural biology.[125]

The types of health complications that might arise when we do venture into these 'unnatural biology' scenarios are unknown, but if you've invested so much money in prolonging your life, I imagine the final exit will not be graceful but a desperate fight to the very end – and that will require even more money.

AMORTALITY WILL NOT BE EQUITABLE

But even if there are breakthroughs in life-extending drugs and they become commercialized and relatively affordable, then another problem arises.

If we extrapolate our current generational demographics around the world, we know from countries with ageing populations that there is an immense strain on a country's economy, as well as on families.

Consider that most social security schemes are designed in pyramid fashion, betting on there being more young people around to fund the schemes than older ones dependent on them. If older people are sticking around for longer, these models break down, begging the question – who is going to pay for the aesthetic and medical treatments required to maintain your endless youth? Who has the foresight to plan for an indefinitely prolonged retirement? How can economies with a surplus of old-age dependents stay afloat, let alone grow?

---

[125]Peter H. Diamandis and Steven Kotler, 'We are nearing "longevity escape velocity"', MarketWatch, 25 February 2020. Available from: www.marketwatch.com/story/we-are-nearing-longevity-escape-velocity-where-science-can-extend-your-life-for-more-than-a-year-for-every-year-you-are-alive-2020-02-24

The World Health Organization already calculates a dependency ratio projection (the number of working-age people for every older person). Based on UN population projections, the world's least developed countries will go from having approximately 16 working-age people for every older person to around 4 by the end of the century. In developed countries, this ratio is less pronounced: 3.7[126] people of working age for every older person, and this will fall to 1.9.[127]

Looking after the sick and elderly who live for decades beyond their normal life expectancies will drain money out of the economy as well as place additional strain on healthcare services.

Quite apart from the financial practicalities, I shudder to think of the dynamics of an extended family gathering, which will include not only great-grandparents, but also great-great-uncles and aunts, as well as their living-longer sprogs.

Catering for these family gatherings will be a nightmare, in terms not only of the volume of food required but also the very real prospect of intricately detailed dietary requirements, which are bound to become more niche and specific when more people try to maintain extended lifespans.

Natural, organic and nutritious food needed to feed the amortal body will be rare, and very expensive. That is, if we still have a planet that can support natural, organic and nutritious food sources. The way the human race is currently treating Earth, I'm really not sure if I want to live on an overpopulated

[126]United Nations, Department of Economic and Social Affairs, Population Division, 'World Population Ageing 2015', 2015. Available at: https://www.un.org/en/development/desa/population/publications/pdf/ageing/WPA2015_Report.pdf

[127]Toshiko Kaneda and Carl Haub, 'How Many People Have Ever Lived On Earth?', PRB, 23 January 2020. Available from: www.prb.org/howmanypeoplehaveeverlivedonearth/

planet that is choked with human detritus and battered by climate change and the extreme weather that will ensue.

This brings me to the concept of hedonic adaptation, as explained by Professor Laurie Santos, the Yale University professor who lectures on 'Psychology and the Good Life', which is proving to be the most popular course in the university's 300-year history.

Hedonic adaptation, also known as 'the hedonic treadmill', is how our brains are wired to return to a set level of happiness despite spikes in happiness. For example, buying and driving a new car will bring limited joy. After a relatively short space of time, the car transitions from proud obsession to just another mode of transport. The brain adapts to something pleasurable very quickly, so once the novelty wears off, it seeks another fix. If you're going to extend your life by another half century or more, hedonic adaptation will not necessarily guarantee a happier life.

The lure of amortality is like the call of the sirens. Conceptually it sounds wonderful, but the practicalities and reality will be very different, even disastrous. Ninety might very well be the new 50, if the Methuselah Foundation are successful with their life-extension therapies, but personally. I'm not sure I want to have to keep working after turning 100, just as some kind of vanity project. At some point, being kept alive with multiple – and guaranteed, very costly – therapies would be just a different version of being kept on life support. Would we really be happier living longer?

Like a perpetual 'groundhog day', the road to amortality will turn out to be a hedonic treadmill: a very long detour to the same destination. And the journey won't be a pretty one, should humanity continue on its current trajectory. The prospect of living in an overpopulated (in the last 100 years alone, six billion people were added to the planet), polluted, environmentally compromised and inequitable world is not one I would relish.

I'd rather stick with my natural life contract, but pledge to work harder at being mindful of it and learn to savour and appreciate it. Throwing money at alleviating disease and improving quality of life for mankind are worthy causes.

Clouding those good intentions with ego and vanity are not.

Imagine if a cruel twist of fate befalls the nudging-on-ancient 1 per cent who, preserved like salted codfish, gradually become wistful and envious of the shorter, but more wide-ranging, lives of the natural lifespanners?

Be careful what you wish for. The road to hell is paved with good intentions.

19

Building an AR commons: Fixing the (Future) Operating System of Life

By John Koetsier, journalist, analyst, futurist

As augmented reality rewrites the future operating system of life, negotiating inter-operating system compatibility will become as important – and high stakes – as negotiating global geopolitical trade and treaty agreements is today. In this essay we explore the potential – and the importance of developing a collective commons – for the operating systems our lives and livelihoods run on.

Augmented reality (AR) is the operating system of the future. Not just of computing, but of life.

We are currently starting to paint default reality with data, insights and entertainment. Right now we do this in slow, small, painful ways: pointing a physical device at a space and infusing our view of it with virtual augmentation. When we shift from smartphones to smart glasses, this will only accelerate.

It's pretty clear to most that the future is smart.

From games to street directions to metadata, and from industrial heads-up displays to workspace information – our new augmented and mixed realities are becoming hyper-aware, data-rich, multi-contextual, and socially interactive. Right now, we see only a tiny piece of that through the small rectangles in our hands or clunky, unsightly objects like Microsoft's HoloLens and the overhyped and under-delivered Magic Leap 1 (a 'wearable spatial computer'). That will change over time as the hardware side of the technology industry does what it does best: make things faster, better, smaller.

But there's a core problem with the future operating system (OS) of life. And no hardware upgrade will fix it.

Today, augmented and mixed realities are temporary, contingent experiences with almost no permanent existence. They're different in every app and on each platform. Some might be anchored in an AR cloud to some landmark in default reality, which is a step in the right direction. But every other AR cloud is ignorant of them, creating a fractured meta-reality. Imagine if, in building the Internet, Dr Tim Berners-Lee created different internets with separate sets of websites for each web browser, all in their own little worlds, disconnected from all the other splinternets.

That's the infant world of AR today.

Welcome to fragmented realities. Welcome to AR darknets: dark by design.

What we critically need is a set of common shared layers of augmented reality, just like we need common layers of physical reality. In default reality, emergency alerts, signage and public notices tend to follow local, national or international standards so they convey information equally to all: readable, understandable, efficacious. We have precisely the same need for persistent consensus existence of data and metadata in a new AR commons... plus myriads of layers of mixed realities with different access and privacy levels for friends, families, companies, organizations and affinity groups. And we need them across apps and across platforms. Building the AR commons is one of the most critical tasks today to shape the world of tomorrow.

Mobile has conquered our time. Whether communicating, playing, searching, locating, learning or just consuming, mobile has eaten the majority of computing time. After doubling since 2013, mobile has also conquered almost 70 per cent of our digital media time. Mobile usage surpassed desktop in 2015, and we now spend an average of five hours a day on apps and the mobile web. The reason is clear: convergence of utility created convergence of activity. Email, web, phone, games, Google, music, videos, banking, retail, news, education: your phone handles them all.

But the future looks a little different.

While smart digital platforms of the future will follow the phone in converging all media upon themselves, they will add a new twist. Not only will they embody all existing media, they will make media of all existing reality.

We're seeing early hints at that in AR-enabled apps on smartphones. With home furnishing apps from IKEA, smart measuring apps like MeasureKit, public art in Snapchat and apps like Sky Guide AR mapping insight on to the night sky, physical reality has become malleable, contextual, intelligent. But despite the magnetism that smartphone screens hold – and five hours/day looking at little screens in our hands is a long time – most people won't go through 90 per cent of their waking hours looking at the world through their screens.

At least, not yet. Not until the next major revolution in computing platforms.

Augmented reality of the future will be a 10–15 hour/day phenomenon via light, stylish and powerful computing on your face: smart glasses.

Need a TV? Here's a virtual one on the wall.

Looking for info on what to do in Boston today? Annotations and suggestions will decorate your view.

Need the top priorities for your work group? They're floating in the doorway as you enter the office (assuming you need to go into an office at all, post COVID).

Want the schematics for the jet engine you're fixing? They're superimposed on the actual engine in front of you. Make reality conform to augmented reality, and you've done your job.

Looking for amazing works of virtual art in real spaces? Add an art channel to your approved list.

Want to play a social game with strangers in a public space? There's one already in progress that you've never seen. Subscribe and you're in.

The applications are literally infinite, limited only by our imaginations.

Of course, not everyone will wear smart glasses initially, especially those who don't need eyesight correction. But as many as 75 per cent of people need glasses anyway, and the benefits of ubiquitous hands-free information, computing, context and insight across basically your entire visual field will, at some point, outweigh the reservations of most.

Smart glasses will be our (desktop/laptop) computers, they will be our theatres, they will be our digital assistants, they will be our portable music systems. In short, they will converge virtually all media on to themselves. Eventually, they might be contact lenses; at some point we may consent to having electronic eyeballs inserted in our flesh. Regardless of the form factor, the ultimate utility remains.

Most critically, smart glasses will enable simple, seamless and wireless mixing of physical and digital realities.

And that will make AR the OS of how we experience the world. But all isn't well in our current reimaging of reality.

Houston, we have an AR problem.

We see it already. The future is coming.

Apple's ARKit and Google's ARCore are giving mobile developers simple ways to mix realities today. Microsoft's HoloLens and Meta's short-lived head-mounted display gave us a taste for how natural it will be to layer virtual objects and information on to and into base reality. And glasses featuring screens like Kopin's, Vuzix's, North (recently bought by Google) and Epson's Moverio will eventually enable simple ubiquitous digital context in analogue surroundings.

But what we see in each of the hundreds of ARKit and ARCore apps is different.

That makes sense for IKEA, and it makes sense for some AR games. I don't really need the whole world seeing how that sofa fits into my living room, and a single-player video game doesn't really need social or a specific tied-to-reality spatial context.

But there's some amazing augmented reality art being created in Snapchat. It'd be wonderful to see that art in whatever app you happen to be enjoying augmented reality in. Google's AR stickers from Disney – now part of the Google app Playground – are potentially cool, but we'd probably like to see ones that other people have tagged on objects in our paths, not just our own.

And wouldn't it be great to arrive at the office and see your co-workers' recent work activity on the wall? Or get a note from a friend as you step into a new restaurant, suggesting you try her favourite dish? Think multiple layers or filters of augments on top of default reality with metadata decorating default data. Think art layers, political layers and sports layers. Work layers, friend layers, family layers.

But this won't happen unless we can find a way to connect separate universes of metadata.

The problem is clear: everyone is building an AR internet. Like the early days of railroads with incompatible gauge lines, no one is focusing on synchronizing the experience. Sturfee is building an AR cloud for cities; Google's Street View is the beginning of a 1:1 digital/physical mapping of the world; Apple and Facebook have related projects; Niantic is building an AR image of the world as a gaming platform and potentially more; YOUAR is building persistent social experiences; Dent Reality is building indoor maps with digital augments. And so we're fragmenting augmented reality by design, ghettoizing augments to small, contingent audiences in separate unlinked apps.

Currently, reality bubbles are dangerous enough, fraying the fabric of society as left and right (and parties of all kinds of different persuasions) increasingly access different 'facts' from different voices and live in essentially different realities. In one, Donald Trump is a heroic saviour. In another, he's a demonic traitor. But at least we have default reality to fall back on in person. In future reality bubbles, default reality and the evidence of our eyes passes through filters of our own devising before entering our eyes.

Don't want to see homeless people? Edit your reality filter.

Don't like a particular political party? Erase all mention of it from your perception.

Download the objectivism filter for an Ayn Rand view of reality. Install the environmental filter for a resource consumption and wildlife preservation perspective. Install the Republican or Liberal or Socialist Party filter to see news, life and cities through party-sponsored glasses.

The power and the capability to do so is decades in the future, even if rudimentary smart glasses exist now, and higher-order smart glasses from giants like Apple, Google and Facebook will ship in the early to mid 2020s. But the system architecture that could ensure the existence of a base layer of consensus reality – even in constructed augmented reality – is something we need to invent now. Without this, we further split our societies.

We need an AR commons to help fix splinter-realities. Something like this would include the ability to:

- Catalogue realities
- Create a publicly available catalogue of AR artefacts and experiences
- Share realities
- Make AR experiences available to any AR app or OS via API
- Enable personalization
- Create a permissioning functionality that any app or platform can hook into, so we don't enter hyper-reality dystopias
- Enable a creative/consumer economy
- Offer a payments layer so that AR artists and creators get rewarded and attention can be compensated … and platforms benefit too
- Integrate social graphs

- Interface with group and/or social graphs so that AR creators can facilitate group experiences
- Respect ownership
- Understand that augmented realities build on physical realities that have meatspace ownership and respect that foundation for augmented reality economies
- Control and regulate advertising

Left to their own devices, marketers inevitably get noisier and noisier, filling ecosystems with commercial messages. An open AR cloud needs to create space for this while managing it, adding settings for individuals to tune in or out.

An AR commons would create an open, connected ecosystem for augmented reality. It would catalogue AR artefacts, experiences and environments across platforms, companies and apps in a publicly available open-source system and then make them available to any AR-capable device. It would include a base layer of default meta-reality via a Wikipedia-style community organized effort, while also adding functionality for filters that enable subscription at user discretion to family, work, team and other filters.

But who will build it?

A common science-fiction trope is hyper-dimensional spaces that are bigger on the inside than out. Augmented reality will in some sense fulfil this by actually making physical reality more information-dense: augmented with seen (filtered in) and unseen (filtered out) content. Building this without an AR commons condemns us to more and more division into thought tribes of religion and politics and persuasion.

But none of the logos of supporting and founding partners include the massive corporations who are most likely to build large commercially successful augmented reality ecosystems. And this is one place where we cannot allow technology to fracture into an Android versus iOS type of divide.

Which means that, currently, we lack the ability to build the AR commons.

Ultimately, we need the Googles and Apples, Facebooks and Amazons, Tencents and Alibabas of the world to connect and commit to interoperability. The chances of that happening seem slim, but we have seen what organized government effort around things like GDPR have been able to accomplish.

And ultimately, that might be what it takes: political power for technological progress. A bit of a role reversal, perhaps, in the eyes of some. But probably necessary.

20

Homo Augeretis

By Craig Wing, futurist, keynote speaker and doctorate candidate

Are we on the edge of the next evolution of mankind? With the advent of CRISPR, DNA modification and brain–machine interfaces (BMIs), are we, as the *Homo sapiens* species, on the cusp of the next evolutionary stage to *Homo augeretis*? Once we pass this event horizon, will we have collectively surpassed a point towards designer babies, interspecies/robotic inequality and the drive for perfection? Are we at a point of irrelevance or transcendence from the human condition? We've always played 'God' for creation, but not for ourselves; now that we hold the power to change the course of our collective evolutionary destiny in our own hands, we will soon pass a critical phase where we need to start asking 'should we' rather than 'could we'.

Designer babies – or, as I like to call them, *Homo augeretis* (augmented human) – represent a new phase in human evolution, a rapid bifurcation from the naturally selected *Homo sapiens* family tree. I suggest that this term, *Homo augeretis*, could be applied to humans who aren't a result of natural human procreation without medical or scientific intervention. That is, *Homo augeretis* can either have had their genetics altered through any number of antenatal DNA sequencing techniques, including embryo selection or editing, or have augmented themselves post-birth with the addition of mechanical – that is, 'cyborg' – body parts or enhancements, or through biological technology: that is, genetic and epigenetic biohacking.

The first of these augmented humans we know to have been born are the twin Chinese girls Lulu and Nana, who were the result of CRISPR genome editing in October 2018[128] by Professor He Jiankui – this was our 'event horizon', where our collective consciousness realized we could control our human DNA. That said, no one officially really knows when we started human experiments to create what will one day become *Homo augeretis*; the research has likely been going on for decades behind closed doors in nations with scientists and governments with more *liberal* approaches to the ethics of 'playing God' with human embryos.

However, none of this should really come as a surprise: humans have been bioengineering themselves and their environments since the beginning of time, whether through growing grains to be drought-resistant or higher-yield, or domesticating then breeding wolves to eventually become the pet dogs we have today, to that even more shocking trend: chimera creation (there have been reports of lab-grown, human–pig chimeras, dating back to 2017).

---

[128]Jon Cohen, 'The untold story of the "circle of trust" behind the world's first gene-edited babies', *Science* magazine, 1 August 2019. Available from: www.sciencemag.org/news/2019/08/untold-story-circle-trust-behind-world-s-first-gene-edited-babies

Of course, the COVID-19 pandemic only served to accelerate the development of human genetic engineering. After all, there is no guarantee that vaccines will continue to work, or that survivor antibodies will be enough to get the global population to 'herd immunity'. As such, it makes sense that scientists are exploiting more radical ways to protect future generations from potentially devastating diseases, including genetic engineering. The scale of the social and economic cost of COVID-19 has created a tsunami of social acceptance for a variety of interventions, from large-scale state surveillance and contact tracing through to more cutting-edge techniques such as CRISPR and even chimera dabbling that would have been socially unacceptable before. In the long run, it may well be much more prudent to create disease-resistant embryos rather than find retrospective vaccines later on. Take cancers, for example: surely the ethical qualms around genetic editing are far superseded by the potential of eliminating (or at least vastly reducing) cancers and the pain and suffering – never mind the fiscal costs – caused by the dreaded disease.

However, because of the current concentration and geographic distribution of global wealth and power, any discussion about the future potential of genetic editing also needs to take inequality – that is, future access to such life-saving and life-enhancing technologies – into account. The gold standard would be for an international commitment to provide access to embryo enrichment as a standard for prenatal care for all, irrespective of income, to ensure no *Homo sapiens* is left behind. Of course, since we have not even managed yet to secure clean drinking water, let alone basic prenatal care, for all the world's most vulnerable people, the idea of equal access to genetic enhancements as a post-human is unlikely to materialize any time soon.

Historically, this kind of research has been conducted in countries with more 'relaxed' avant-garde regulations (such as China), but post COVID we could very well see an almost global acceptance that medical regulations have to be relaxed to accelerate scientific advances and secure equality for future generations.

Of course, global acceptance of the potential of human editing should be followed by global regulations to safeguard what 'enhancements' are within acceptable parameters. There needs to be recognition that 'playing God' is dangerous. That said, *failing* to use the technology we have available to us to prevent health threats (such as another, perhaps more devastating pandemic) that could wipe out humankind, is perhaps a greater risk to humanity at large. (Of course, on the flip side, allowing widespread investment in genetic engineering could also open humanity up to genetically tailored bioweapons, designed to target a particular DNA profile.)

Potentially sensible genetic enhancement global standards could, for instance, include limiting increases in IQ to no more than 15 basis points (cognitive enhancements), or limiting increased oxygen levels to 10 per cent (physical enhancements), eliminating age-related conditions (eyesight deterioration, cholesterol, sugar levels, dementia), and setting upper limits for the 'feel good' chemicals in the brain (serotonin, endorphins, oxytocin, dopamine). There are many, many more possible regulations we could consider, but these are the main areas where I foresee that unchecked enhancements could result in serious social, economic and geopolitical conflict. Of course, regulations or no regulations, there will always be black markets and rogue states (typically, failed economies with scant oversight, regulation and unethical leadership), where these regulations are easily bypassed, with potentially destabilizing outcomes.

The reality is, CRISPR-type technology, unlike nuclear technology, is very cheap and fairly easy for even non-scientists to dabble with. Essentially, 'open source' genetic code will soon allow practically anyone with enough time and money to edit their own bodies, or even, more distressingly, to utilize the technology to develop DIY weapons of mass destruction. Imagine placing the bioweapon equivalent of an atom bomb in the hands of every angry teenager around the world…

Unfortunately, there is no real way to put the CRISPR genie back in the bottle.

That devastating scenario aside, I suspect social conflicts around genetic inequality will be the most likely flashpoint we face. Humans are, and have been historically, incredibly intolerant of even minor differences (as can be attested by tribal, racial and gender conflicts across the ages). I cannot but think that *Homo sapiens* will likely treat the first *Homo augeretis* even worse than we have treated those minor differences within our own root species. I foresee a world where *Homo augeretis* have to fight for the right to vote, the right not to be discriminated against in the workplace and the right to marry, intermarry and procreate, just like countless other minority groups before them have had to do through the history of civilization.

Conversely, augmented humans could use their enhanced strength and intellect to set themselves up as a 'master race': that is, wield their genetic power to oppress and rule over their genetically 'normal' *Homo sapiens* cousins. Of course, if already enhanced *Homo augeretis* decline to intermarry with *Homo sapiens* and use their advanced DNA and intellect to further enhance their own offspring and so on, within just a few generations the distinction between *Homo augeretis* and *Homo sapiens* would be almost impossible to bridge.

Now, as we stand on the precipice of the bifurcation of humanity between naturally selected and intelligently designed subspecies, I hope we as humanity can reflect on the far order consequences of the decisions we are making today, specifically:

1 The ability to create *Homo augeretis* must be made as economically viable, quickly dispensed and thoroughly administered as possible. Any delay in doing so will increase all kinds of inequality and allow for those with ill intent to create further divisions.

2 Although decentralizing access to human enhancement is undeniably important, we also need to think through the consequences of DIY biohacking where our natural inclination is for self-improvement – in fact, that is part of the reason we evolved naturally: to better ourselves compared to our peers to stand a better chance of survival and societal success. Ironic, that we may be on the precipice of *Homo augeritis* evolving at the expense of *Homo sapiens* through the creation of a new kind of inequality and possibly even the emergence of an undeniably biologically and mentally 'superior' race.

3 We need urgently to have a global conversation about the ethics and access to self-biohacking (that is, postnatal genetic manipulation), since the technology already exists and will become increasingly difficult to control and prevent. Perhaps we should even host a global referendum on the way forward; the geopolitical consequences of a nation being left behind, if the rest

of the world embraces the potential, will be nothing short of devastating. That said, we need to look at the potential benefits as well as the harm – after all, humans have been doing a form of biohacking/enhancements since the beginning of time: clothing, tools, hearing horns, glasses. Then it went internal: pacemakers, stents, hearing aids and, a decade ago, brain–machine interfaces. Why should subcutaneous enhancements be the 'uncrossable' line?

4 The final and most important point is that we should not be so focused on asking 'could we?' that we never pause to ask 'should we?' Could we create a world where we can create *Homo augeretis*? Yes. Should we? Well, that depends... there are always unintended consequences of good intentions. The emergence of practical human genetic engineering has set us on a path where we must ensure we all (*Homo sapiens* and *Homo augeritis*) realize there isn't an 'us' versus 'them' path or one predicated on divisions, superiority and elitism.

Yes, it's likely *Homo augeritis* will have more advantages, more opportunities, maybe even a better 'life' than their naturally selected counterparts. Yet, much like even today, future genetically modified humans should not be treated in a way that disenfranchises or disqualifies them from society. Indeed, individuals who choose to edit and enhance their DNA later in life deserve the dignity, rights and kindness we extend to those who choose to alter their appearance or gender today.

No, rather we need to find a way that we can flex ourselves and our minds to learn and complement each other.

Life has always been unequal; it always will be. That's a fact. What is different, this time, is how we choose to respond – not react. One is emotional, based on fear and focusing on the differences and the 'or'; the other is logical, based on understanding, and focuses on the 'and'. This is one of those times where we need wisdom, kindness, humility – and even forgiveness.

PART FIVE

Over The Horizon

BACK FROM THE FUTURE

Over the course of this book we have taken you on a wide-ranging journey through the near and not so near future. Our authors have shared their dreams and nightmares. If we have done our job, you are now equal parts inspired, depressed, excited and scared about the future of humanity. Yes, there is much about which to be concerned in what lies ahead for the future of our species, but there is also good reason to be hopeful about where we are headed as we learn to transcend the limits of our minds, bodies and physical environments. There is little debate that, despite the spectre of climate change and the reality of poverty and inequality and all our other wicked problems, there has seldom, if ever, been a better time to be born in terms of life expectancy and quality of life.

Our job is to make sure that the future we are leaving behind for our own descendants is better, broader and more brilliant than the one we inherited from our parents. Our children and their children deserve broader horizons, not shrunken dreams tarnished with hauntology. This means we need to stop mortgaging a future that does not belong to us in order to satisfy our present desires. It means we cannot use more than our fair share of Earth's finite natural resources. It means we must find ways to do even more with even less. It means that it is our duty to find ways to achieve both growth *and* sustainability, for surely our children should not have to pay for our choices with their futures.

This in turn requires shifting our time horizon from the immediate present to *the long now*. The long now is a concept that futurists use to describe the roughly 200-year-long rolling period each of our lives will touch as we pass each other like ships in the night. The long now period stretches back in time from the present to the date the oldest person alive was born; and forward in time to the future date the youngest baby born right now will eventually live until. If we, as individuals, organizations and nations are able to shift our thinking to consider the impact and consequences of our choices over this full long now period, we will begin to make better, more sustainable decisions. There is a Greek proverb that says: *A society grows great when old men plant trees whose shade they know they shall never sit in.*

This idea has been beautifully brought to life by Norway's living library of the future. The library is in fact a forest of one thousand trees planted in 2014 with the purpose of being cut down and turned into books 100 years in the future, the year 2114.

The future library forest (or book incubator), which is situated in Oslo, Norway, contains enough trees to print 1,000 copies of 100 never-before-read books (at least one of which was authored by dystopian futurist Margaret Atwood). The future book manuscripts are written one per year for every year between 2014 and 2114. After completion, each original manuscript is carefully stored in a secret 'silent room' hidden on the top floor of the Oslo library, where they await printing in 2114, when the trees the books will eventually be printed on will be ready for their metamorphosis.

What a thought: planting trees you will never live to see grow tall, writing books that will not be published within your lifetime. I see the project as a love letter to the future souls who will one day take their place in our world.

There is something truly beautiful about living in the *long now* and planting seeds that will only be reaped by future generations.

We need more of this: more foresight – and less selfish obsession with the short now.

It's this sort of selfless intergenerational thinking that will eventually see human civilization breach the limits of the Earth's atmosphere and (literally) head for the stars.

We may also then be able to rally together to dream, design and perhaps build the contemporary equivalent of the ancient intergenerational projects we once faithfully promised our descendants. Think of Gaudí's la Sagrada Família, which has been under construction since 1882 and is only expected to be completed in 2026. Imagine what we could yet achieve with that sort of long-term selfless mindset. Long now thinking is the only way we will eventually deliver on the fine future ideas we were once promised.

It's our duty, ours and yours, dear reader, to break the present-bias trap of postalgia and to turn the hauntology of the future we have been denied from science fiction into science fact. We have the technology and tools to do exactly that, but are we brave enough to step up and build that world? Or are we too distracted by our present problems to see past them towards the future that we desire and deserve? Surely not. Surely there are enough of us who refuse to settle for the small future of pointless conspicuous consumption, wasteful, expensive energy production and frankly broken, obviously rigged financial and political systems that we have been handed. Where are our perpetual energy machines? Our personal flying cars? Our robot butlers? Our cures for cancers?

The future challenges presented in this book are just the beginning. As we wrote in the introduction, a futurist's aim is to change the future, not to predict it. We have hand-picked a selection of the issues that keep us up at night; however, there are many more pressing issues that need a champion to change. Now we hand that challenge over to you, the reader – our challenge to you is that if you are not comfortable with any of the futures presented in this book, or if there is some other future trajectory that you are growing concerned about, you need to go out and change that course.

To help you do just that, we have prepared a beginner's guide to the future on the following pages, which will help you consider the essays and issues presented in this book in the same way as a futurist would.

The Beginner's Guide to The Future

Understanding trends and likely trajectories, such as those presented in this book, allows us to look at the possible and probable future ahead.

One of the tools futurists use to make sense of the future is the futures cone, as described in Nikolas Badminton's chapter, 'Start with Dystopia', at the beginning of this book.

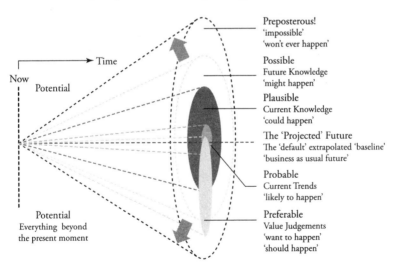

Essentially, the further ahead we look into the future, the fuzzier the picture becomes, hence the cone-shaped visual metaphor. From our current perspective, the further ahead we try to anticipate, the less clear our vision becomes. In times of rapid change, of course, that cone of possibility becomes wider, and the future becomes more uncertain.

That said, longer-term trends are more predictable than short-term trends. Once we cut out the noise of short-term news and shiny fads, and are able to zoom out and see the bigger picture, quite often it becomes easier to see the general direction the world is headed in.

We can use foresight to understand what is more likely to occur and to consider what is most desirable to happen next.

We start with considering the most probable future trajectories, which represent the continuation of the current trends described above. This represents the most likely future we can anticipate based on what we currently know.

Next, we broaden the cone to consider the plausible range of possibility – in other words, what could happen if the current trends explored accelerate or decelerate.

Then we widen the range of our view even further to cover the full set of possible futures, this time encompassing realistic but unlikely breaks in current trends. At this widest view, we discount nothing. (This is the level where we should include eventualities such as a pandemic or an asteroid hitting the Earth.)

Lastly, we change focus from probabilities towards preferences, and consider our preferable future, which may not necessarily be the most probable future destination. (It is also important to note that your preferable future may not be a preferable future to someone else. Your preferable future is what is best for you, your business and your organization.)

We encourage you to think about each of the issues presented in this book in turn, using the future cone tool to imagine what is likely to progress in each of the trajectories outlined, and to explore the limits of the possible – both desirable and undesirable – outcomes you could end up facing as an individual, or as an organization. Again, the essays in this book are meant to open conversations, not to close them. This book is just the starting point of the ever-shifting future.

Of course, as we've said, the aim of all these futures exercises is ultimately to *change* the future – that is, mitigate threats and take advantage of possible opportunities – rather than to simply predict it. The goal is to use the futures cone to broaden your perspective and develop a clearer picture of the ever-widening gyre of the future; to understand what is probable, what is possible and what is preferable – and then to inspire considered change.

We hope that the questions, opportunities and concerns our authors have raised will help you to define the futures you want to live in – and the futures you want to avoid. If we can just get more people to ask more questions, and challenge the nature and sense of the future options on offer by our local, corporate and international leaders, then we will have accomplished our mission.

After all, getting more people to think about the outcomes of the decisions we make for ourselves – and the decisions made on our behalf – allows us to interrogate the wisdom of those choices. Choices affect different groups and different individuals differently; this is why we need more voices debating the merit of the ideas and ideologies that are defining our shared futures.

All choices have constraints (or trade-offs); and all choices have consequences (some of which can be very far-reaching indeed, causing untold collateral damage over space and time). It's *complex* out there. We live in an open system. Everything and everyone is connected. Even simple decisions can cause large amounts of chaos. Think of the old woman who swallowed a fly, and then a spider to catch the fly, and so on... Quite often our attempts to solve wicked problems end up making those problems even worse, as the cure can be more deadly than the disease.

This is why thinking about the future like a futurist requires taking the time to work through the second, third and nth-order future effects of your present choices. And to consider the desirability of those effects, not just for yourself, but for the fellow humans who share your contemporary and future timelines.

Yet thinking about the future from the luxury of the present is not just good for avoiding disasters for humanity in general, it's also good for business.

When we think about the future before it arrives, we have the luxury to make proactive rather than reactive decisions. This can be a serious source of competitive advantage in the face of a crisis or short-lived opportunity. That is the real advantage of investing in future thinking: it buys you time when you need it most.

Individuals and businesses that can see past the immediate future to the long-term future have a significant head start compared to those who are stuck in reacting to the endless present.

(If the future seems more overwhelming than exciting right now, and you need some help exploring the far limits of what is possible, in a positive, proactive way, head on over to the Future Starts Now Foundation, on the next page, and we will help find the perfect futurist to fit your personal or professional objectives.)

You have no excuses. Go out and change the future.

About the Future Starts Now Foundation

The Future Starts Now Foundation is a loose federation of 'anti-futurists', including all your authors here, interested in changing the course of history to be better for everyone. The Foundation helps businesses and individuals with the information, insights and ideas they need to go out and change the future for themselves. We need more people pushing for more, different, futures; there is no one-size-fits-all future.

We invite you to join us. Visit TheFutureStartsNow.com for more information.

Find a Futurist

Andrew Vorster, innovation consultant and futurist (UK)
Web: andrewvorster.com
Twitter: @andrewvorster

Anne Skare Nielsen, chief futurist at Universal Futurist (Denmark)
Web: www.universalfuturist.com
Twitter: @anneskare

Arsam Matin, Founder, Gen Z Futurists
Web: genzfuturists.com
Twitter: @arsamfuturist

Bronwyn Williams, futurist, economist, trend analyst and partner at Flux Trends (South Africa)
Web: whatthefuturenow.com
Twitter: @bronwynwilliams

Cathy Hackl, futurist, technologist and VR specialist (US)
Web: cathyhackl.com
Twitter: @cathyhackl

Chris Yiu, Executive Director of the Technology and
Public Policy team at the Tony Blair Institute for
Global Change (UK)
Web: yiu.co.uk
Twitter: @clry2

Craig Wing, futurist, global speaker and doctorate
candidate
Twitter: @wingnuts123

Dali Tembo, Afrofuturist and founder of The Culture
Foundry Co (South Africa)
Web: culturefoundryco.com
Twitter: @Dali_Tembo

David Tal, Founder and Strategic Foresight Lead at
quantumrun.com, a world-leading futures research
agency (Canada)
Web: quantumrun.com
Twitter: @davidtalwrites

Dion Chang, founder of Flux Trends, South Africa's
most well-known and well-respected trends and futures
consultancy (South Africa)
Web: fluxtrends.com
Twitter: @dionchang

Doug Vining, business and technology futurist and partner
at Futureworld.org (South Africa)
Web: futureworld.org
Twitter: @dougv

Duena Blomstrom, keynote speaker, author, co-founder and CEO of Emotional Banking™ and PeopleNotTech Ltd™ (UK)
Web: duenablomstrom.com and peoplenottech.com
Twitter: @DuenaBlomstrom

Kate O'Neill, futurist, founder of KO Insights, author and professional speaker (US)
Web: KOInsights.com
Twitter: @kateo

Kristina Libby, futurist and CSE at Hypergiant (US)
Web: KristinaLibby.com
Twitter: @KristinaLibby

Leah Zaidi, award-winning futurist and the founder of Multiverse Design, a strategic foresight consultancy (Canada)
Web: multiversedesign.com
Twitter: @Leah_Zaidi

Manish Bahl, leading futurist at Center for the Future of Work at Cognizant (India)
Web: cognizant.com/futureofwork/author/details/manish-bahl
Twitter: @mbahl

Mathana, tech ethicist, philosopher, academic and futurist (Germany)
Web: twitter.com/automationomics
Twitter: @StenderWorld

Nikolas Badminton, global futurist, researcher, speaker, and media commentator (Canada)
Web: nikolasbadminton.com
Twitter: @NikolasFuturist

Steven D. Marlow, leading technologist focused on behaviourism, cognition, the philosophy of other minds and the future of thinking machines (USA)
Web: medium.com/@sd_marlow_72794
Twitter: @sd_marlow

Theo Priestley, anti-futurist, technologist and keynote speaker (UK)
Web: theopriestley.com
Twitter: @tprstly

Index

Note: page numbers in **bold** refer to diagrams.

INDEX